MW01520311

RECLAIMING YOUR INNER CHILD: WOUNDED OR NOT

HOW TO BREAK FREE FROM THE PAST WITH THE
POWER OF LETTING GO THROUGH LOVE AND
ACCEPTANCE TO FIND PEACE, BALANCE AND
LIBERATION FROM POWERFUL EMOTIONS

FAYE MACK

© **Copyright 2022 - All rights reserved.**

The content contained within this book may not be reproduced, duplicated, or transmitted without direct written permission from the author or the publisher.

Under no circumstances will any blame or legal responsibility be held against the publisher, or author, for any damages, reparation, or monetary loss due to the information contained within this book, either directly or indirectly.

Legal Notice:

This book is copyright protected. It is only for personal use. You cannot amend, distribute, sell, use, quote, or paraphrase any part, or the content within this book, without the author or publisher's permission.

Disclaimer Notice:

Please note that the information contained within this document is for educational and entertainment purposes only. All effort has been executed to present accurate, up-to-date, reliable, complete information. No warranties of any kind are declared or implied. Readers acknowledge that the author is not rendering legal, financial, medical, or professional advice. The content within this book has been derived from various sources. Please consult a licensed professional before attempting any techniques outlined in this book.

By reading this document, the reader agrees that under no circumstances is the author responsible for any losses, direct or indirect, that are incurred due to the use of the information in this document, including, but not limited to, errors, omissions, or inaccuracies.

SPECIAL BONUS!

WANT THIS BOOK FOR FREE?

GET <u>FREE</u>, UNLIMITED ACCESS TO IT AND ALL OF MY NEW BOOKS BY JOINING THE FAN BASE!

Scan with your camera to join!

CONTENTS

INTRODUCTION

In today's world, it's too easy to get lost in the droll existence of punching the clock and coming back home exhausted from the day. Pop a lasagna in the oven and eat it in front of the television. Go to bed worn out and wake up dreading the new day. Rinse, repeat. If this sounds familiar, you may have lost touch with your inner child.

The fact is, as an adult, you take on responsibilities— responsibilities to your job, your family, your bill collectors. You feel an overwhelming sense of getting lost in this tide. It can be hard to hear the child inside crying out for attention, but they're there, and they are demanding that you slow down.

Losing touch with your inner child takes on a lot of different facets. For instance, have you lost that inquisitive nature about the world? Do you no longer get unapologetically excited about your passions? Do you even know what your passions are anymore? These are all problems that trace back to losing that childlike inner spark. This book is an attempt to give you the right tools to rediscover that child within.

With that inner light dimmed, you might find yourself struggling with self-expression. Of course, it's not a terrible thing to grow up. As we learn, being an adult *does* mean more freedom. It means more knowledge. However, without that childlike wonder that this book will help you harness, you might feel a sense of being 'stuck.'

You're stuck in a world that seems to be drained of its once vibrant colors. This book is an attempt to inject those colors back into your life, to bring back that childlike wonder that you have found yourself lacking. With the proper study and implementation, you might find that you are more excited by the world around you.

This book strives to be a step-by-step guide for finding that inner child, taking them by the hand,

and leading them into the light of your everyday life. You will learn how to get to know them, and to understand what has kept them in the dark for so long. Perhaps it is just the new pile of responsibilities that you have found yourself buried under. Maybe it is because at some point in your life you were wounded, and it doesn't feel safe for that child to come out anymore.

Whatever the reason, there is hope. This book is designed to help you get back to a place where you can release that inner child without fear or without second guessing yourself. Not only have these steps helped me in my path to reclaiming that spark, but I have seen it work for countless others. Their stories and wisdom helped sculpt this book into what it is— an uncommon guide to bringing out that inner child, and to liberation from powerful and unaddressed emotions.

That's not to say that this process is without its discomfort and setbacks. I have made numerous mistakes along the way. Much of what is written here came from trial and error. And then some more trial and error. It is, after all, part of all science to fail and try again. I believe that making these early mistakes gives me a stronger foundation from which to talk about these things. I have seen what works, and I have seen what has not worked. My knowledge has been molded and informed by these mistakes, and has made me a fiercer advocate for this type of work.

The formula at which I have arrived has helped many people reclaim that spark of joy that their inner child protects. I want to see the same happen for you, which is why I am glad that you have chosen this book and made the first step in this journey. Honor that decision and see this through. (You already have the book, after all.)

Doing this halfway will not serve you. You want to be all in when you pursue this. Give it some time and watch as practicing these steps aids you in rediscovering your inner child and all that they have to offer you. It is an important endeavor.

The most important thing to realize from reading this book is the importance of rediscovering your inner child. The concept can be traced all the way back to famed psychiatrist Carl Jung, who defined the inner child as that free-spirited, forgiving side of us that still feels childlike joy. However, the flip side of this coin is that they also carry the wounds that we have experienced. This can make it difficult to coax them out of the shadows and into the light.

Though it might be a difficult task to start, especially if some of those wounds are still fresh, there is great benefit to this practice. Some of these benefits include:

- Boosting your self-esteem
- Discovering the root of harmful patterns you have developed
- Tapping into your fun, creative side
- Incorporating self-care into your daily routine
- Seeing the world through eyes of wonder
- Harnessing your creativity

Rediscovering the child within can bring up some ugly scars, but it can also help you learn how to really tackle the things that trouble you. It opens doors to better ways of living. There are many who have implemented the steps outlined in this book who have gone on to lead more fulfilled lives.

For instance, a woman we will call 'Rachel' rediscovered her passion for art in the process of rekindling that inner light. When she was able to get in touch with her inner child, she was able to heal some of the old wounds, but used those lessons learned to inform her art. Though she is by no means a famous artist, she found a purpose to living that has brought her the joy she was searching for.

There are many more stories like this, but I won't regale you with each one. You will see for yourself what you can accomplish as you move forward in this journey. First, though, I have a question for you: Are you ready to break out of your current existence and find a new way of living? This book is a stepping stone to a life better lived, and by following these simple practices you will see a remarkable differ-ence. You just have to be committed to the journey.

I will take you by the hand and walk you through each step. So, have no fear. You are not embarking on this journey alone. I have walked this path and I know how weird and uncomfortable it can feel. However, I also know how to walk people down this path as I have done it before. I have felt the weird emotions that stir up when pursuing my inner child. I have done the hard work. I understand what it feels like to stand on the other side and look back at my progress.

It's imperative that you take these steps to heal your inner child. In doing so, you will find that you are healing unaddressed emotional issues within yourself. That child carries wounds that you are acting out in your everyday life. To break the patterns, it's important that you lead that child by the hand into the light and embrace them as they are.

This process can be a lot of fun, but it can also be difficult. Do not lose heart as you go through these steps. You might open up some old wounds that you have been ignoring for some time now. It is important that you are aware so that you can face them head on with no blinders.

No matter what your journey looks like, it is commendable that you have begun it. You are seeking out healing for your inner child and that can only help you grow as a person. Make sure to check in with yourself regularly as you do this and see how the growth has changed you. The results might surprise you.

I hope this book brings you some hope. I hope it is the start of a lifelong journey to really understanding that inner child. I have no doubt that by following these steps, you'll live a fuller, more rewarding life. Read on to unlock your inner child—

and everything that they can teach you. You might be surprised at the results.

1

IT FEELS WEIRD...WHY?

IT MAY FEEL WEIRD AT FIRST

Okay, so you have picked up this book, meaning that you have recognized the need to embrace your inner child. However, it might still find kind of weird to consider. Even the language can feel uncomfortable. The concept might seem alien if you haven't begun this journey yet. Have no fear. You are not alone. Many find it strange to embark on this journey. That is okay. It is natural to feel uncomfortable when starting something new, especially something as strange as this.

It can feel weird to us because we have been taught that to be an adult is to be responsible, and children are often the antithesis to this. However, it is all about balancing our heart's needs with the demands of our adult lives. Embracing your inner child doesn't necessarily need to mean that you quit your job and begin your life as a circus acrobat. Those are dreams of a child, and it's okay to let them go. After all, your inner child might need some parenting from your adult self. We will get to that later.

More than being like a child, embracing your inner child is accepting that there is a childlike spirit within us, wanting to get out. That childlike spirit is playful, kind, and full of wonder. When it has been suppressed, we might find that we are locked into a life that lacks wonder and excitement. We also might find that we don't fully understand our own emotional reactions.

The fact is, our inner child informs much of what we do, whether we are willing to accept it or not. It is better to embrace this child and learn to understand them than to lock them away in the corners of our minds. It opens up doors for us to fully understand ourselves and heal the wounds that need healing. So, think of it more as a practice of self-care.

I am not asking you to do cartwheels down your cul-de-sac or get really into finger painting. I am not asking you to shirk responsibilities. I am asking you to acknowledge the innate state of wonder that has been locked away inside of you. Taking these first steps might feel strange and alien, but they will ultimately benefit you. You just want to let go of the preconceived notion that childlike pursuits are silly or frivolous. In fact, they are the key to reaching out to your inner child and healing any wounds that might be present.

Approach this process with grace, for yourself, and mostly, for the child you once were. Think about it for a moment. We are often our own harshest critics, but when it really comes down to it, there are few among us who would act harshly in the face of a child. The same should be said for your own inner child. With a gentle and understanding approach, you can push past the 'strangeness' of the process and really reap the benefits that come from embracing your inner childlike spirit.

WHAT THE INNER CHILD IS NOT

The inner child is not an age regression. It is not returning to a place of no responsibilities. It is not acting with petulance and impatience, as many children do. When you start this process, you might be wondering what an inner child is and *isn't*. So let's take a closer look at the ins and outs of embracing that childlike wonder that you might be lacking in your life.

It is important to understand the distinction between embracing your inner child and acting like a big kid. Although these things can, at times, coincide, you don't have to live in a place of perpetual immaturity to fully embrace your inner child. It is more about coming to a place of acceptance than anything.

Our inner child, simply put, is our subconscious true self that has been present since we were young. It is often associated with innocence, hopefulness, and wonder. It is a part of our being that is delegated purely to childlike thoughts! This can look like the wonder we feel when we see twinkling lights on houses at Christmas. It can be the unbridled excitement we feel when experiencing something new.

However, a wounded inner child can also carry the baggage of trauma and grief. If, as a child, you were taught to deny certain parts of yourself in order to receive love, then your inner child might still be weighed down and hiding away their true feelings. That is unhealthy for both your inner child and the current adult that you are. So, start unpacking those feelings now. You will be better off for it, I promise.

Reclaiming your inner child can be a more difficult process when you have been wounded in childhood. However, it is still a beneficial process to fully understand yourself. It involves coaxing out that child and relearning our emotional responses. You might find yourself unusually closed off, or, on the other side of the coin, very reactionary in your emotional responses. This can be traced back to wounds accumulated in childhood.

Some people associate the inner child with immaturity. While there is nothing wrong with purported 'immaturity' from time to time—think buying plushies, coloring, doing a cartwheel—it doesn't have to be about these practices. It is more about a state of being; namely, opening yourself up to those formative practices. Whatever your childhood was like, there are benefits to allowing your inner child out to play from time to time.

Now that we have covered what an inner child *is*, it's important to put to bed some misconceptions around the concept. These misconceptions are at best silly, and at their worst, harmful to the healing process.

Some people hear the concept of the inner child and believe that it is a separate personality, outside of ourselves. This misconception can be scary, as it calls up an image of disorders such as dissociative identity disorder, where one has multiple personalities living within their one body.

This, however, is not the case. The inner child is not something separate from your primary personality. In fact, it can be considered the very core of your personality. It's where the very essence of who you are is derived. That's why it is so important to avoid neglecting it.

Others believe that "inner child" is just another term for immaturity. This is also not the case. Though children are often immature, there is a wisdom to the things that they do that we can learn a lot from. For instance, children are spectacularly good at staying in the moment. They are not thinking about the next thing they have to do. They just enjoy the moment for what it is.

Similarly, children are easy to get along with and quick to make friends. Their spirit is light and kind. Their gentle ways of finding their way into people's hearts is not just admirable, itis something we could do well to return to, on some level. Gone are the days of sharing a juice box, but maybe next time a coworker is heading for a coffee, you could offer to cover them and head out with them on your break.

With a wounded or neglected inner child, you might find yourself at best uninspired and at worst, reactionary and depressed. Being able to make peace with this side of yourself is not about combining two personalities. It is about finding the seed from which your growth has sprung and deciding to water it.

BARRIERS TO FREEDOM: SOCIETY, SELF-CONSCIOUSNESS, SHAME, AND TRAUMA

When you begin this journey, you might be at a disadvantage. You might find that there are barriers blocking you from truly embracing your inner child and the wonder that they promise. We will break down some of these obstacles and determine what you can do about them, should they arise. None of them are insurmountable, and the fight through them is worth the rewards on the other end of the battle.

Whatever your obstacle (or obstacles), you can take heart in knowing that this is a worthy cause. You will begin to see your life truly flourish when you understand and accept the part your inner child has to play in your life.

Taking a look at each obstacle one by one can help break down what each one might mean for your personal situation. They all come with their own set of challenges, and thus should be addressed differently.

Society

As we're well aware, we live in a society that has grown cynical and divisive. All you have to do is log onto Facebook and you are bombarded with that cruel truth. Because of this, we might feel pressure to conform to this same mindset. We were taught about peer pressure in school, but back then, it was all about people offering you drugs. (This turned out not to be the prevalent problem we were taught it would be.) Instead, however, I see that peer pressure does exist in adult society and it is the pressure to "act your age."

Do not mishear me. You should definitely be acting your age and taking responsibility for your actions. However, sometimes society misconstrues what that truly looks like. Adulthood and cynicism become synonymous, and those who reject the notion are looked down upon. Because of this, we might be reticent to take these steps for ourselves.

I encourage you to reject the current landscape of cynicism and criticism. It can be hard, especially when we are an innately social species. However, you will find that cynicism and negativity do not serve you as well as you might think. They are protective measures that are better left in the past. So let them go and walk into the light. There is so much you can learn from your inner child.

There is no clear-cut answer to this phenomenon. As you become more in tune with your inner child, however, you will start to realize that the opinion of a larger society becomes less important to you. That's not to say that you will become a contrarian, either. You will simply see things through a new lens. So take heart; there is hope on the other side of this obstacle.

Self-Consciousness

Maybe it isn't society that is making you second guess the work of reclaiming your inner child. Perhaps it has a lot less to do with what others think of you and how you, yourself, view the concept. Are you too cool for your inner child? You might be resistant to the language used, feeling as though it is an infantilizing way of viewing yourself. The whole thing might feel a little ridiculous.

The best way to dispel this particular obstacle is with added knowledge. Though "inner child" has become a bit of a buzz word in modern psychology, it's not without merit. It is a legitimate and scientifically-realized phenomena about your psyche. The fact that you are resistant to it is, in itself, evidence that you can benefit from reconnecting with your inner child. There is a part of you that is shying away from the vulnerability necessary for such a practice. This can point to an inner child that carries wounds.

Unpacking those wounds and better understanding your formative thoughts can greatly benefit you. But I get it—the thought of connecting with your inner child sounds ridiculous. Even uncomfortable. You are perfectly comfortable with the present, and don't wish to return to a time when you were young and vulnerable. This is where you might benefit greatly from therapy and trauma work. If and when you decide to seek out a therapist, try to find one that specializes in this type of work. It can do wonders for old wounds and leave you feeling a hundred pounds lighter.

Don't be your own worst enemy. Embrace that original sense of wonder that you entered this world with. Do the hard work and come out the other side a more complete version of yourself. Leave the cynicism and doubt in the past. It is worth it, I promise.

Shame and Trauma

For so many, shame and trauma are full stop obstacles, and this is hard for me to wrestle with. Truly, those who benefit the most from this type of experience are those who have wounded inner children—those who have been through Hell and carry the wounds on that part of their mind. A wounded inner child can shy away from the light.

It is about coaxing them into the light and trying to fully understand them. By understanding those wounds, you can better understand your decision making as an adult. A wounded inner child can look like reactionary behavior, or on the polar opposite end, a very closed off demeanor.

Whatever it looks like in you, do not let it stop you from embracing this journey and finding the light on the other side. You are not defined by your trauma, and your shame serves no purpose. Practice some self-compassion and find that you are stronger than you would have believed.

Working through shame and trauma from our pasts can be a difficult process, but it is necessary to the work of discovering the inner child that resides within our consciousness. I understand the difficult road you face, as it is one that I have walked myself; but the other side is beckoning, and it is a much better place to thrive.

It is time to break the chains of trauma and learn a new way of living. Though it may never leave you, you can live a life outside of the effects of trauma. You can begin a new life on the other side. I have faith in you that you can make the necessary changes in your life and find a better life on the other side of your shame and trauma.

EMBRACING THE LIBERATING TRUTH

I cannot stress enough how important it is to recognize your inner child and nurture communication with that side of you. The benefits are nearly endless and well documented. Those who have embraced their inner child and learned to explore the depths of their psyche come out the other side more curious and optimistic, choosing to see the world through a brighter lens.

The benefits don't end there. It is not just your lens that changes. You will also find that you walk through life with a different attitude and a different way of tackling the problems that you confront day-to-day.

One major benefit of embracing your inner child is that you will find a new sense of resilience and perseverance. After all, children are a resilient bunch. Have you ever watched a baby beginning to learn to walk? They stumble and fall and then get right back up. They don't stop to ponder the concept of walking or worry about their purpose. They just get up and try again. Returning to the mindset of a child can help us view the obstacles in our paths as something to overcome, rather than something that is blocking us from our destination.

You might also find that along with this new sense of perseverance, you become more adaptable. The two often go hand in hand, after all. Children learn to get by with what is available to them. They often have to deal with schedule changes and new experiences, and they just take it as it comes. However, as an adult, you may have noticed that you have become set in your ways. The slightest change in schedule can throw you off for an entire day. Listening to your inner child can help you "roll with the punches," so to speak, and move forward with less anxiety surrounding these last-minute changes.

Furthermore, you might find that you are less rushed in your life. Children have no sense of urgency. They dawdle, they stop to look at a cool rock they found, they talk endlessly about the dream they had last night while their tired parent desperately tries to get them to eat breakfast. While I'm not telling you to take it to any kind of extreme (please, still show up to work on time), I am showing you that opening up this door in your psyche might allow you to finally slow down and smell the proverbial roses.

These are only some of the benefits of getting in touch with your inner child. We will touch on some others as we go further in this book, but to whet your appetite, here are a few more benefits to taking these steps:

- You will begin to dream bigger
- You will find that you are kinder to others
- You will have more fun in your life

- You will find you are more active
- You will find joy in the small things

However, there is another side to this coin. While there are many benefits to accepting and healing your inner child, there are also drawbacks to *not* doing so. It is important to understand these negative impacts that neglecting your inner child can have as we move forward in this book. It illustrates how imperative it is that you start taking this seriously.

For starters, being disconnected from your inner child can leave you feeling what Pink Floyd coined "Comfortably Numb." You are disconnected from your own life and the lives of others. You might not feel in touch with your own emotions or even know how to vocalize what you are feeling. This can lead to problems with yourself and with your relationships.

Furthermore, you might find yourself more easily overwhelmed or discouraged than those who are in touch with their inner child. Your self-esteem might not be in the best shape, leading you to worry that you can't handle life's challenges. This feeling of being overwhelmed and discouraged can be daunting and exhausting. Taking a step back and asking our inner child what they need can make all the difference in this scope.

Alternatively, you might deal with a lot of anger. This anger is coming from a neglected inner child who was never given the chance to heal from the wounds inflicted upon them. As mentioned before, neglecting your inner child can make you very reactionary with your emotions, and often, this comes out in anger. You might find that you lash out or resent others.

You also might notice that you lack enjoyment in your life. You are stuck in a rut and every day just runs into the next. You have forgotten when you last felt a spark of pure joy. This can be an easy red flag to miss, as you might think that's how adult life is supposed to be. However, this couldn't be further from the truth. Life is meant to be enjoyed to the fullest, and it's possible, should you choose to heal that inner child and truly connect with it.

There are many benefits to embracing your inner child and countless pitfalls to ignoring them. I hope that understanding this gives you a new drive to pursue this important journey. You have already taken the first steps in learning about this concept that might be somewhat foreign to you. Keep that momentum going and read on! This book will give you all the tools you need to unlock that inner child and tap into the limitless potential they can offer you.

Do not worry. I will walk you through the steps you need to take in order to make it to the other side. There are steps both difficult and fun that you can pursue to fully unleash that inner child.

THE BOTTOM LINE

Though delving into the deep end of finding your inner child can seem a little strange at first, it is well worth the benefits it will bring you. Let go of the voice in your head that says this is silly or shameful. Let go of the expectations that society has put on you. In this process, you answer to yourself first— not 'society.' It is not their journey, and they do not get a say in your healing.

Avoid misinformation surrounding the inner child. There are many who have taken the concept and turned it into something that it was never meant to be. Fully understanding what the inner child truly is can break you out of that self-consciousness and help you to see things as they truly are.

Do not let misinformation and doubt hold you back. This is important work that will find you ultimately fulfilled. Your doubts and self-consciousness need to be left in the dust as you pursue this newfound freedom. Once you have rejected these feelings of self-consciousness, it is time to explore what the inner child truly *is,* so that you can find your way to them. The next part of this book will outline what this looks like and give you a clear picture of how to bring out self-compassion for your inner child.

Read on if you would like to continue this adventure. You have already tackled one of the hardest parts—dealing with your inner demons and doubt. The rest of the journey will be, at times, challenging; but at other times, full of joy. Pursuing these steps will bring you closer to the inner spark that your inner child represents.

2

THE PART OF YOU THAT NEVER GREW UP

WHO IS THIS INNER CHILD?

The inner child has been a buzz word in modern psychology lately, but that does not mean that this is, by any means, a new concept. As mentioned earlier in this book, this idea was cultivated by the famed psychologist Carl Jung in the early 20th century when he was developing what was coined as "Jungian archetypes."

Jung rejected the idea that we entered the world as blank slates. Instead, he argued that humans have predestined "primordial images" within their subconscious. These images take on the form of certain archetypes. This might sound a little hoity toity, but bear with me.

These archetypes, developed by Jung in 1919, were defined as innate, unspecific knowledge which prefigures and directs conscious behavior. "The child" was among these archetypes, forming the early phases of the inner child concept. The child was seen as the "potential future" and the beginning of developing personality.

So what does this all mean? To put it more simply, Jung believed that there was a part of our consciousness that represents a child, the early stages of our development informing our future course of action. This archetype that he defined was the beginning of the development of the inner child concept. However, it was far from the end of this concept. Other psychologists took this idea and developed it further, adding to the already revolutionary idea.

This concept of the inner child was expounded further upon by psychologists and writers in the years that followed. One of the most notable examples is the husband and wife team, Vivian and Arthur Janov, who went on to publish books on the subject titled *The Primal Scream* (1970) and *The Feeling Child* (1973).

This inner child is your base personality, the consciousness with which you started. It is not some mystical entity or ideal. It is just a term for what we began our lives with. This inner child can shift through the formative years and become "wounded" due to neglect or abuse, but your inner child is still, at its core, the true essence of who you are as an individual.

FINDING THAT INNER CHILD

What you might be asking now is, "What now?" I've given you the background on the concept of the inner child, but so far, we have not gone too far into how to help that inner child walk into the light of day. It can both be fun and challenging to draw out that inner child, and with the right tools and knowledge on your side, you can reap the benefits.

To start with, you will want to keep an open mind. This can be difficult if you have lost touch with your inner child. As I mentioned earlier in his book, cynicism is a prevalent problem in today's society. I argue that this is one of the greatest barriers to finding your inner child and allowing them to come out and play. Try to remain open not just to what you read in this book, but to any further information you might find on the matter. Even in general, an open mind can do wonders for coaxing out that childlike spirit.

Secondly, look to actual children for guidance! Believe it or not, children are filled with wisdom that can do well to learn from. They are experts at finding joy in the small things and remaining in the moment. (When was the last time you were fully present in the moment without worrying about your to-do list?) You can also benefit from their sense of playfulness.

Maybe you don't have a child or even *know* a child whom you can spend time with. That's fine. Try spending some time in childish pursuits. Color in a coloring book, play with a puzzle toy, or spend some time watching children's television (I recommend *Girl Meets World* completely unironically). Do something that brings you back to that childlike mindset. You might find you uncover some childlike wisdom while you follow those pursuits.

It might also be helpful to return to some of your childhood memories. Go through old photos or childhood mementos that might spark some memories. Reach out to your family members and even childhood friends if you are still in contact with them. Ask them to tell you stories about that time of your life. Listen and try to return to those memories.

Now, I understand that this can be difficult if you experienced a tumultuous childhood. Your inner child might be wounded. In this case, it can be difficult to return to childhood memories when they carry pain along with the wonder. Still, it can be beneficial to return to those memories. You might find that you will learn things that can help you begin the process of healing those old wounds that you have carried into your present. You just have to do a little bit of walking on eggshells to find the memories that serve you as they should.

These simple practices are great ways to begin the process. It simply cracks open the door for that inner child to be able to look out. Struggling with these steps is completely normal. Though they may seem simple, they can prove difficult when you have been neglecting your inner child for some time. Conversely, you might find that these practices are easy for you. Great! That means your inner child was not as distant as you may have thought! This is good news.

LOVING UNAPOLOGETICALLY

When approaching your inner child, it is important to do it from a place of love. Children are sensitive, and your inner child is no different. Showing them some love and care can do wonders for its ability to come out and explore the world around you. This might feel weird, especially if you are struggling with self-esteem or woundedness. However, it is an imperative step. You must show your inner child love unapologetically, regardless of what state they may be in.

This can be difficult for a number of reasons. We covered some of them earlier. Society, shame, and self-consciousness can act as barriers to unapologetic love. However, you need to remind yourself of the importance of the work and lean into this emotion. Your inner child is no doubt craving this kind of understanding.

You need to maneuver around the obstacles in your path and realize that love trumps any societal concerns or self-conscious notions. This process is life-changing, and it's imperative that you realize that, coming at it with everything you've got. That includes shedding some of that self-doubt and fear.

When you are beginning this process, unapologetic love is the best tool you have available to you and it costs nothing. Remind yourself of the enthusiasm and unabashed love you experienced as a child and try to bring some of that into your life.

Love is important to any relationship, and the relationship you have with yourself is no different. In order for your inner child to feel safe, they need to feel loved and wanted. So, speak lovingly and gently to them. Show them the compassion you would show a real-life child. It could make all the difference.

This can be a difficult process when you have been wounded. A fearful inner child is the most needing of love and the hardest one to offer love to. We are a product of our environments and experiences. If you were taught at a young age that love was dangerous, love can be hard to give and accept.

That just means you have to give it all you have. Work through those feelings of neglect and fear, reaching across the distance to tell your inner child you love them and that they are safe with you. It's not unlike trying to speak with a child who is actually scared. You need to be gentle and kind. Show understanding for the fear and the pain they have experienced, and invite them to express what they need to express. Doing so might be difficult, but it is well worth the effort.

This is when healing comes into the equation. Making peace with the past is an important factor in healing the inner child. Once you have found a way to deal with the wounds of your formative years, you will find getting in touch with your inner child is a much easier practice. That's what this book is here for. I will take you by the hand and walk you through the steps necessary to healing those old wounds that have kept your inner child locked up.

WHY SHOULD I LET IT OUT?

Now, you might be asking, "Why is this so important?" After all, you've been managing, thus far. But do you want to just get by, or would you rather flourish? There are many benefits to letting out your inner child, which we covered earlier in this book. It can encourage us to look at the world with a kind of wonder, it can boost our confidence, and it can allow us to see the world through a more creative lens.

Though those are great reasons to allow your inner child out, they aren't the end all be all of healing. Rather, consider your earliest experiences. You might look back at hard times from your childhood with adult eyes and judge or invalidate the emotions you felt. We belittle our own pain. However, as the famous author John Green put it, "Pain demands to be felt." If we do not deal with our earliest wounds, they will find ways to crop up in our adult life.

Looking at those early wounds with childlike eyes means looking upon them with no judgement and no belittling. For that child, those wounds were big and they were meaningful. We may have stripped them of some of their sharp edges as we got older, but they are still very real. They still inform how we operate.

Connecting with the inner child is all about returning to a time of innocence. It's about healing those old wounds and making room for childlike wonder in your life again. It might seem silly when you begin the journey. It might feel unnatural. But, it is, at its core, about healing.

Healing is a powerful word and I do not use it lightly. When I say that this can be a healing practice, I mean it. You might find that you can set down the baggage from the past and experience life with a new lens when you embrace your inner child. This is a sign that old wounds are stitching themselves back up. You are letting down some of that baggage.

Without true love and compassion for your inner child, you are not fully loving yourself. It is, after all, a part of you. It is a part of you that wants to feel understood and accepted. Letting it out might mean you're more playful and open to the world around you. However, it also means that you are a more complete person, willing to accept all aspects of yourself without apology.

ADULTING HAS ITS CONS

When we were children, many of us couldn't wait to be a "grown up." We wanted the freedom and autonomy. However, adulthood is not all it's cracked up to be. Without being too much of a downer, there are negative aspects to 'adulting' that can weigh down our spirits. There are bills to pay, chores to do, and groceries to buy. Sometimes, we can find ourselves stuck in a rut.

So many of us get lost in the shuffle. We rush from one thing on our to-do list to the next, without much time to stop and smell the proverbial roses. We have developed a type of chronic tunnel vision that blinds us to the wonders of the world around us. We only see the goal that is in front of us and we don't always take in the beauty that surrounds us.

These aspects of adulthood can leave us feeling drained and uninspired. At worst, they can leave us feeling anxious and depressed. I know that I have struggled with that from time to time. Times when there is so much to get done, that we don't have time for things like fun and self-expression. It can be a real bummer. That's just another reason that connecting with your inner child is so important. You want to keep your spirit light and unhindered.

Breaking out of a dull existence and embracing the enthusiasm of a child can shake things up in your life. It can open doors that you had thought were closed and give you a whole new perspective on life. This might feel foreign at first, but the benefits of viewing the world in this new way are too valuable to put a price on. You just have to trust in the process and feel your way through to the other side.

So where do you start on this journey? Now that I have regaled you with the mechanics of the inner child and why it is so important, you might be wondering where to go from here. The most important thing you can do is to acknowledge that this is a necessary step. The second most important step is acknowledging the moments that have brought you to this point.

THE BOTTOM LINE

The inner child is, as we've covered, a part of us that remains unblemished from our experiences. It is the true essence of who we are. With that understanding, you can begin to build an atmosphere around yourself that is welcoming to this part of you. Above all else, love that part of yourself, because it is often the most neglected piece of ourselves we carry around.

Let's face it—adulting is not a rose garden. We spent our whole childhoods waiting with bated breath for the chance to be an adult, and we soon discovered that there's a lot involved that we don't necessarily love: going to work, paying bills, balancing a checkbook, and dealing with our range of emotions. Through connecting with your inner child, you can better make it through these moments with a new perspective.

Letting out your inner child can be difficult, especially when early wounds are present. However, done right—and with compassion—you can live a fuller life as you show up for your inner child every day. Taking the chance can be scary, but you have to admit, it is tempting as well. Acknowledge the pain they still feel today and reassure them you will never leave them.

The next step we will go into is acknowledging your childhood. You might be dreading this chapter, as there are painful memories there, but I promise, it won't be as scary as you fear. There are steps you can take to ensure that you pursue this route in a healthy and safe way. I will guide the way. You will find some closure and hope on the other side of this. I promise.

3

ACKNOWLEDGING YOUR CHILDHOOD

TRAUMA BURNS

This is one of the hardest chapters to write, and one of the hardest lessons you will learn in this book: Learning to make peace with your childhood. This can be particularly difficult when you add trauma into the mix. Unfortunately, there are few adults living today who had a rosy childhood. Generational trauma is a real thing and has likely been passed down to you.

The point still remains that to nurture and reparent your inner child, you must face the past—warts and all. This includes any possible trauma that you might have locked behind a door in your mind. You might have to go exploring in some dark places, but on the other side is a more balanced life.

As a child, you most likely had no say over the things that happened to and around you. You were a passive participant in your own life, and therefore, there are likely unaddressed wounds. Facing them and understanding them is vital to the process of getting in touch with your inner child.

Childhood abuse and neglect can show up in a lot of ways in our adult lives. We are, after all, a sum of all of our experiences. We might not even realize that we are experiencing the lingering effects of this abuse and neglect. Denial is a powerful thing.

However, unhealed wounds from our childhood are powerful and wreak all kinds of havoc on our adult brains. This can look like attachment disorders, reactionary emotional states, and lack of stability. Because we lacked that attention or stability in our childhoods, we act out the responses in our adult lives, even when the danger has passed.

This is due to the fact that we never addressed these early wounds. Once they have been recognized and dealt with, you can begin the healing process. However, this involves letting that inner child speak and tell you how they are feeling. Listen closely, because you need to better understand where they are coming from to get a handle on these trauma burns.

Depending upon the severity of the trauma in your life, I might suggest taking this step with a licensed therapist, who can navigate you safely through those tumultuous memories. Their guidance will be vital in processing those complicated emotions without triggering yourself. There will be a portion in this book that will walk you through how to find an appropriate therapist for your situation.

IS IT ALRIGHT TO GRIEVE?

When you delve into your childhood, you might discover that there are some times for which you need to grieve. You may need to grieve the childhood you were not allowed or grieve things that you went through. This is natural, and it's absolutely okay to spend time grieving these things. In fact, it's a vital part of the process.

Grieving is a natural part of human existence. We grieve the end of relationships, we grieve the death of loved ones, and we grieve sudden changes. So, what does it look like to grieve the childhood we didn't get to have? That can be a little trickier, but when confronted in a healthy manner, it can be liberating.

Grieving is all about saying goodbye. That means you need to look back at your childhood and say goodbye to what could have been. This can be difficult, and at times, really rough. However, grieving in a healthy way is imperative to moving on and moving forward. You need to put the past to bed to learn what it can teach you.

So, let's talk about healthy ways to deal with that grieving process. For many of us, we have never been taught how to grieve in a *healthy* way, and that has left us stunted. So, in order to really discuss this grieving process, I feel it's imperative that we go through myths surrounding grief and dispelling them.

Myth: Ignoring the grief will make it go away quicker.

This one is a huge misconception. Many choose to shove down those feelings because, after all, they are uncomfortable. They are hard to deal with. However, avoiding those messy emotions will not make them go away. They will just resurface at a later time, likely in an unhealthy way. It's important you deal with those emotions head on.

Myth: You must "be strong" and "put on a brave face" in the face of your grief.

This is a narrative that has been informed by general society. Crying and showing emotions are seen as a weakness, and we tend to internalize those preconceived ideas. The fact is, though, that crying and talking about those emotions are actually healthy. You are allowing your body to express what your mind is going through. It's a release, and it is extremely beneficial to the grieving process in the long run.

Myth: Moving forward with your life means forgetting about your loss and pain.

Once you've worked through the cloud of grief, it will be time to move forward with your life. This might feel uncomfortable and disrespectful to what you are grieving. It is not. It is a natural part of the process. If you have dealt with your grief in a healthy way, you should be able to move forward. It does not mean the pain is not still there. It does not mean that what happened does not matter. Instead, it means that you are healing. You are learning to cope with that which caused you grief. Embrace it.

Now that we have dispelled some of those general myths, let's get into the nitty gritty of dealing with that complex grief. This is not for the faint of heart so strap in. We are going to do some difficult work.

To begin with, you will want to acknowledge the pain. Acknowledge the grief. Get familiar with it. Understand the facets of it. What about your childhood makes you feel these emotions of grief? Acknowledging that this pain exists can be a difficult process, but it is vital to move through those emotions.

Next, you will want to accept that acknowledging this pain might bring up new and unexpected emotions. You might find yourself feeling sad, angry, and confused as you wade through the waters of this grief. You need to accept that these feelings will churn up within you, and make peace with them.

Understand that your grieving process will look different from mine, your friend's, etc. Grief is always unique to the individual, so don't play the comparison game as you make your way through this process. Just because you aren't responding in the same way as someone else doesn't make it an incorrect response. It just means that it's how *you* respond to grief. As long as your reactions are healthy, don't worry too much about how your grief looks in comparison to others'.

Also, it's important that you don't go through this grief alone. Seek out the support of those in your life as you go through this grieving process. Call up a friend and meet them for coffee. Talk about what you are going through while you process these complex emotions. There's no sense in walking through this alone if you don't have to. Having that added support will greatly benefit your journey.

This might also include seeking out a therapist, especially if the wounds you experienced in childhood were severe. They can safely navigate you through this process without triggering you. They went to school to learn how to help people manage complex emotions, and unpacking childhood grief falls under that umbrella.

Finally, support yourself as you go through these emotions by taking care of your body. This might sound like common sense, but body wellness and mental health go hand in hand. Make sure you are drinking enough water, eating healthy food, and getting the proper amount of rest. Grief is taxing on the body, and you need these things now more than ever. Go a step further and really nurture yourself. Take a nice long bubble bath with candles lit, or take a walk with your favorite playlist. As you delve into these difficult emotions, find ways to take care of your body and mind at the same time.

Whatever form your grief takes, lean into it and feel these emotions. Realize there is a difference between grief and depression. Grief is a process, and is something that you can work through by taking the appropriate steps. You will not be in the dark forever.

Healing those early wounds starts with acknowledging and grieving what was and what simply wasn't. Give yourself permission to do this. Give yourself permission to feel whatever you need to feel so that you can move forward into the light on the other side of this pain.

JOY—IT'S ALRIGHT TO ENJOY THE EXPERIENCE

On the other side of the coin, you might not have any heavy wounds to deal with. Perhaps your childhood was healthy and enjoyable. You have very little, if anything, to heal from. That's great! This book is for you as much as it is for those who have experienced childhood trauma.

If your inner child is not wounded, just hiding out, then this experience will be a lot more fun. It's okay to take joy in the process! You don't have to feel guilty for your healthy and fulfilling childhood. In fact, I encourage you to revisit it and revel in the love you have for it.

Revisit that childhood and remember what about it brings you joy. This can be a fun practice, and one that will open the door to releasing your inner child. Return to old memories that bring you nostalgia and joy. What was it about those moments that brought you peace?

Perhaps it was the feeling of safety or not having as many responsibilities. Maybe it was cool summer nights when you'd stay up late with your friends, watching the stars. Whatever those moments are, use them as a lodestone to guide you back to the inner child within.

It's important to recognize your childhood as something that brings you joy. It is important to embrace those positive memories, as they will be your tether to guide you back to your inner child. Those positive memories can lead you back to a place where you are able to feel like that kid again, and that's a great thing! Loving your childhood is a blessing, and understanding that is imperative and positive in this process you are undertaking.

There might be a sense of guilt when you revisit your childhood, knowing that so many others were wounded in their own. Try not to dwell on that. Though it is unfortunate what others have suffered, you don't need to carry their burden as penance for the blessed childhood that you had.

Let this joy and wonder regarding your childhood guide you through the steps I have outlined in this book. You might find it easier to connect and nurture your inner child, and that should be something of which you are glad. I think you will find that even you have a thing or two to learn about letting out your inner child though, so read on.

BEING YOU FOR YOU—DON'T ALTER THE TRUTH OF YOUR CHILDHOOD

It is important that you are honest about childhood when you delve into the past. There are those who do not want to be left out of the discussion and invent wounds that are not actually present. This can be harmful, both to your journey, as well as to those who actually experienced those wounds. Be honest with yourself about how your childhood affected you.

Don't belittle any wounds that might be there, but also don't go looking for wounds that don't exist. Being completely honest with yourself about the wounds or lack thereof will give you a better picture of the work you need to do. Don't feel pressured to have baggage that you don't. Instead, be grateful for what you had.

You might feel somewhat left out of the discourse, but at the end of the day, this is good news! Whatever guilt you may feel over not experiencing trauma in childhood should be left at the door. I mentioned earlier that you are more than your trauma. You are also more than your good experiences. You have strength that lies outside of trauma and pain and that is admirable as well.

Whatever your childhood looked like, there is hope for you finding your inner child. Making peace with or appreciating your childhood is just the first step. There is still work to be done. With better understanding of these tools and strategies, you will be well on your way to reclaiming that inner spark of the inner child.

THE BOTTOM LINE

Understanding and coming to terms with our past is a difficult but necessary part of this process. Whether you had a traumatic childhood or a relatively blessed one, you want to look at it with the eyes of adult and see it for what it was. If there are wounds that need to be healed, get to work healing them. If you were able to make it through childhood without trauma, celebrate that fact and embrace it.

Understanding our childhood for what it was is a lot easier to do as an adult than it was when we were children and did not have the knowledge we have now. You can look back at that period with a critical eye and perhaps even some compassion. Whatever it looks like for you, there is hope on the other side.

As we move through these chapters, you might start to doubt and overthink. This is common, especially for adults in today's day and age. It just needs to be tempered with some good old-fashioned mindfulness, which I will walk you through in the next chapter. You've got this.

4

DIAGNOSING THE WOUNDED INNER CHILD

AM I OVERTHINKING?

As humans, especially as adults, we tend to overthink everything. Consider the last time you had to make a decision. Did you agonize over every detail and alternative? Congratulations, you are an overthinker. There is a club you can join and I am a member. The problem with overthinking is that we tend to doubt and second guess our own pain. This can be harmful for a number of reasons, but it begins with belittling the wounds we are carrying around with us.

Overthinking is harmful to the process of dealing with the emotional wounds that our inner child has experienced. If you catch yourself overthinking the pain you feel, stop and give yourself some grace. Don't belittle the pain. Pain *is* pain, and if you experienced it, then you need to come to a place of calm acceptance rather than tying yourself up in knots overthinking it.

Our bodies are truly incredible machines that hold something of a memory card. Our bodies remember trauma; they remember pain. When your brain wages war with your body, trying to convince it that the pain isn't *that* bad, you set yourself back.

For instance, perhaps your family was a relatively healthy one, but you lived in poverty. You look back and think, "Well, I wasn't abused. Therefore, it wasn't that bad." However, living in poverty can cause great stress, even when we are young and don't quite understand the implications of it.

Maybe you went through a terrible loss when you were a child—a friend, or a family member. Though this is a natural part of life, those wounds still exist and are trying to tell us something. Overthinking can dissolve the healing process by getting us turned around, reconsidering and revising history.

When you allow yourself to think as a child would, you will start to realize that this comes easier. After all, most children do not have the worries an adult has. They are free to face one day at a time, not over-thinking every step. Embrace that side of you and relinquish your death grip on having to examine and reexamine every facet of a situation.

This is where practicing some mindfulness can do wonders for you. There's been a lot of talk about mindfulness in recent years, but the question remains—what is it? Mindfulness is staying present in the current moment. There are a number of ways to do this. Here are a few that might be helpful in your journey to stop overthinking everything.

- Body Scans: Check in with your body. Go through each body part and identify the sensations that are present. Do you feel tension, pain, comfort? Being aware of our own bodies can keep us from straying too far into our manic thoughts.
- Breathing Exercises: Also helpful for anxiety, breathing exercises are great ways to slow down that train of thought that has gone off the rails. Try square breathing to start. It is a simple practice where you breathe in for four seconds, hold your breath for four seconds, and then let it out

for four seconds. Try this for a few breaths and really try to bring your mind back to the present.

- Counting Colors: This one can seem a little silly but hey, we are attempting to get in touch with our inner child, so silliness seems appropriate. You can relax your body and count everything you see of a certain color. For example, if you choose green and you're outside you can count the leave on a tree, the grass, flower stems, the car that just passed by... Doing this keeps you in the present moment and halts the ultimate spiral from overthinking.

By practicing mindfulness on a daily basis, you can find that overthinking happens less and less. In fact, you might find that you are less prone to anxiety and doubting yourself. These are good signs that you are on the right track. Stop overthinking and start living the life you deserve.

Overthinking is not just the suppressor of the inner child. It is also the suppressor of self-confidence and creativity. Remember that as we continue through this book. There might be ideas you are introduced to that leave you skeptical. It is 100% okay to question things, but don't spend too much time over-thinking when the idea is to let loose a little.

DIAGNOSING—SIGNS OF A WOUNDED INNER CHILD

The concept of the inner child can be hard to wrap your head around. For that reason, you might not realize if you actually *have* a wounded inner child. The idea might seem foreign, and you aren't entirely sure what that looks like. Diagnosing a wounded inner child might seem complicated, but there are actually clear signs that point to this phenomenon. You just have to be in tune with yourself.

If you didn't feel safe as a child, for whatever the reason may be, you might have a wounded inner child, and identifying that is important to your ultimate recovery. So, how do we diagnose this? Simply put, we look at the evidence present in our current state of being.

These wounds can take shape in adulthood in a lot of different ways, but simply put, they manifest in how we present ourselves to the world. Perhaps you have a hard time sticking up for yourself. You don't feel like you can express discomfort or displeasure in how you are being treated. That is the wound of your inner child, demanding attention.

There are various other ways that it may manifest, such as:

- Feeling like something is innately wrong with you
- Hoarding things, and having a hard time letting go
- Feeling driven to always overachieve
- Being extremely self-critical
- Being a rigid perfectionist about everything
- Feeling ashamed of expressing strong emotions
- Not getting mad when you ought to, and when you do, it comes out as rage
- Being extremely distrustful, even of yourself
- Struggling to say "no"

Though these are not always indicative of a childhood wound, they are pretty solid indicators that your inner child is crying out for help. When you identify these problem areas it might feel overwhelming, but do not worry. We are going to deal with these issues as we work through healing your inner child.

Identifying these wounds and addressing them are vital to the process, so try not to feel shame if you identify with any of the items on that list. These are common struggles and need not be cause for shame or guilt. Instead, view them as an opportunity to grow beyond the baggage that you have been lugging around thus far.

If anything, you should be looking at your childhood wounds with a sense of compassion. Would you tell little you that they are bad or ugly? Of course not. So do not treat your trauma and pain in such a way. That inner child hears everything you say to and about yourself.

FORGIVING AND BREATHING

Now that we have identified that there might be some wounds present, the next step is going to be a difficult one. Forgiveness is key in the process. This encompasses forgiveness for the wrongs committed against you and forgiveness for the mistakes you may have made along the way. This can be a challenge, I understand. So, I will do my best to walk you through the process, as the benefits are seemingly endless.

Let's not get it twisted. Forgiveness is *hard*, especially when the wound is deep and sharply felt. When someone has hurt us, it is our natural response to retreat and resent. However, this can keep us locked in a cycle of anger and sadness. Withholding forgiveness can be like drinking poison and waiting for the other person to die. Our unforgiveness rarely affects them as much as it damages us.

So, where does one even begin? This can be the most difficult part, especially when we have revisited our past and we might feel a little raw from the memories. These feelings of anger and resentment can chip away at your own joy, so it is important to be able to let it go.

That's not to say that you can't be angry—that you can't feel the feelings that come with that betrayal. Allow yourself to feel angry, grieve the pain that they caused you, and admit that you have been hurt. This is vital to releasing that built up intense emotional energy. Once you are able to admit that those feelings are there, you can begin to work on the unforgiveness festering in your heart.

Now comes the hard part. Make peace with those feelings and let them go. You might want to write a letter to the person who hurt you and then burn it.

Write a text and not send it. Just get out everything that you need to say in a gush of emotions so that you can begin living outside of them.

Don't worry, though. Letting go of those emotions is not saying that what happened was okay. You are not absolving the other person from responsibility for your actions. You are merely deciding that their actions will no longer direct your course. You are doing this for *you*, remember.

That brings me to my next point—forgiving yourself. This can be even more difficult than forgiving others. We tend to be our own worst critics, and in this regard, it's no different. Forgiveness for ourselves and the choices we made when we were young is no easy task.

The best piece of advice that I can offer you here is something that a dear friend told me—you did the best you could with the knowledge you had at the time. This can seem like a small comfort when you are looking back at a past that is difficult to swallow. However, it's important to understand and internalize. You are not the sum of your mistakes. Do not let them define you. You did the best you could.

Furthermore, you were a child. Children are basically ingrained to make mistakes. That is their whole purpose on this earth, making mistakes so that they can learn and become better adults. Maybe you weren't the best child to your parents. Maybe you even flunked out of high school. None of that matters to who you are now. Forgive yourself, breathe, and move forward.

Dwelling on your past and the decisions you could have made differently does nothing but lock you into unhappiness and discontent. Rather, you should be facing *forward* and focusing on the next step. So, set one foot in front of the other and start walking toward your future.

EMBRACING THE WOUNDED INNER CHILD

Your wounded inner child is crying out. What they are crying out *for* depends on the wounds that were inflicted on them. Childhood wounds are specific to each person, and depending on what you experienced, you will need to approach things differently. There are a large range of wounds, including:

- Embarrassment
- Abuse

- Isolation
- Lack of stability
- Being silenced
- Being despised
- Feeling alienated

These are all things that can have a deep impact on a child and therefore cause wounds that we still carry around with us today. It comes down to addressing these wounds and healing them in a healthy way.

Simply put, you need to accept your past for what it was and embrace it. This does not mean that you have to accept it as okay. Wounds are there for us to heal, not to belittle. These wounds can manifest in your adult life in a variety of ways that do not serve you. These can look like neediness, impulsivity, or even narcissism. These things do not serve you, and in fact, keep you locked in your childhood pain.

To get to know yourself and your inner wounds, pay attention to your inner child. Take some time to try and listen to what it is asking for. You can look at your current actions and emotions and get a better idea of what you are looking for in this healing process.

Furthermore, it might be helpful to take it a step further and actually journal as your inner child. This is especially helpful if you fear that your inner child is childish and immature and thus, attempt to shove down the emotions that they are trying to whisper to you. Put those fears to bed and allow your inner child to say what they need to say.

This practice actually has a two-fold benefit. For starters, it allows your inner child to concretely express their inner thoughts and emotions. It allows them to verbalize what they are feeling and what they ultimately need. Furthermore, it acts as a tracker for your subconscious. You can stay on top of what is going on with your inner child as you continue to journal as if you were them.

The next step might seem like a breath of fresh air. Instead of dwelling in the past, this step focuses more on the present and the things that bring you joy. Simply, surround yourself with positivity. This doesn't mean you stop going to your job, but it does mean making simple steps towards deeper inner peace.

This method is extremely helpful because it is letting yourself know that you now have conscious control over your surroundings. As a child, this may not have been something you could claim. In fact, it most likely was not something you had. You did not get to choose your school or your classmates. You didn't get to choose what house you grew up in, or what family you were born into.

As an adult, though, you now have choices. You get to decide where you go and who you surround yourself with. This reeducates your inner child. It tells them that they are no longer stuck in a situation with no control. They are safe with these positive influences, and it might be the step that coaxes them out into the sunlight.

This leads me into my next point, which is arguably one of the most important. *Protect* your inner child. No matter your age, your inner child will always react negatively to certain stimuli, feeling powerless in the face of it. This is normal. What you need to know, is how to handle this.

It is quite simple in practice, though it can be uncomfortable at first. You need to start setting boundaries, keeping your inner child safe from harmful situations. This might mean you need to cut some people out of your life, if they aren't respectful of your boundaries. I know that sounds somewhat intimidating, but this about your own mental health and the health of your inner child.

This practice is one of self-love and confidence, which are two things you may not have experienced in your early days. That means they can feel uncomfortable at first. However, as you grow, you'll begin to realize that setting boundaries and cutting out toxic relationships comes more easily. Once you see the benefits, you will understand the importance of such a practice.

Now for some fun. Do some things that your inner child used to love doing! Depending on where you are on this journey and how receptive you have been thus far, this can actually be quite easy and bring a lot of enjoyment. As we "grow up," we feel a responsibility to take on adult attributes. This isn't all bad. You want to be responsible. You want to be depend able. However, this also means you may have shoved yourself in a box with your interests, sticking to things that are strictly "adult" in nature, because you feel you should.

Don't feel locked into these pastimes that seem more "respectable." You are the navigator of your own life and you get to decide what you pursue. So maybe, occasionally, you skip out on drinks after work and spend time coloring or playing video games. These activities were important to you as a child, and indulging in them lets them know they are safe.

These all might seem a bit alien, and I can tell you why—you are starting to put yourself first in your own life. In a time when self-care can be called self-ishness by many, it is understandable if these practices make you uncomfortable. However, putting yourself first in this journey is tantamount to success. Be a little selfish and self-serving. Allow yourself to indulge in self-love.

QUITTING THE NOT-SO-GOOD OLD BLAME GAME

While we're uncovering some of these early wounds, you might be feeling the need to point fingers and blame others for the state of your inner child. While this can be applicable in terms of abuse, there are scenarios where this is not helpful to the situation.

The fact of the matter is that a lot of our childhoods sucked. It's just a matter of numbers. I knew very few people who look back on their childhood with no complaints. It might not have been a great situation, but pointing the fingers at your parents can be harmful and ultimately unhelpful.

Unless they were expressly abusive, your parents were most likely just humans trying to do their best with parenting. Though there are a million parenting books out there, there is no Bible for parenting. There is no end-all-be-all of parenting books that walks parents through the process of raising children with absolutely no mistakes. You need to start accepting that maybe, just maybe, they were doing the best they could in the situation that they found themselves in.

That does not mean you don't get to feel hurt or wounded. Your pain is still valid. However, wasting your energy on feeling resentment towards your parents is just a game that no one wins. Blaming others for the pain and frustration you feel is fruitless at best and harmful at its worst.

Instead of playing the pointless blame game, begin viewing your childhood through the lens of grace. It is entirely possible that those who caused you pain did so without realizing they were doing so. I speak from experience, so I'd say I have a bit of expertise in this area.

My parents moved us around every two years. They felt called by God to travel to different states and cities. As a child my life was constantly uprooted, and the cast of people in my life was always rotating. There was no stability. There was no consistency. It has caused a lot of problems in my adult life that I am working to address. When I first realized this wound, I wanted to blame my parents and get angry.

Then I realized, they both came from unstable households. Their understanding of how to raise a family was badly damaged by their own upbringing. They did the best they could. They were loving parents, but they did not know how to create an environment of stability for their children. Instead of being angry, I began to view them with grace. I strove to understand the wounds that *they* experienced that led them to their decisions.

Letting go of the loaded pistol of blame and trying to come to a place of understanding is when I finally started to heal. My anger at them lessened and my anger at the world lessened with it. There was no point in pointing fingers at two hurting people for doing the best they could and ultimately failing. I had to let that go and move forward.

That is what I want for you. Unless your parents were abusive in some fashion, try to remember that they were young and doing the best they could to raise you in the best way they knew how. This might not have been the most beneficial environment in the end. However, holding on to that resentment is a meaningless game that leads nowhere. I encourage you to forgive, breathe, and walk away from the toxic game of blame.

In forgiveness, you are allowing yourself to let go of the no-good resentment that is tying you to your troubled past. There is no place in this journey for resentment and anger. There is more to this life than what has happened to you. There is more to your history than how your parents failed. Remember that as you walk forward.

WHEN IT'S TOO DIFFICULT

I've walked you through some ways to relinquish your past wounds and move forward into the light. Perhaps you took to this easily, or if not easily, at least you were able to take to it at all. However, maybe you have some deep wounds that are too painful to face alone. That is all too normal in today's world, and you are not alone. You don't have to do this alone.

There is a possibility that you have wounds that need extra care. That is okay. Don't feel shame around this fact. You might just need some extra support, and don't we all, from time to time? Seeking out a professional to help you wade through these mixed emotions can be extremely helpful, in this case.

Don't let this prospect worry you. There is no shame in seeking a professional's help. In fact, I suggest therapy to just about everyone. We can all benefit from the help of a professional to wade through the complications of life. So, if you find yourself needing extra help with this process, just know that there is no need to fret.

We are all broken people in some way or another. We all carry wounds of some kind, whether from childhood or adulthood, and being able to unpack that baggage with a nonjudgmental party can be incredibly freeing. I, for one, enjoy going to see my therapist, as I know I will have a safe place to talk about what has been plaguing me lately.

As important as seeking out a therapist is making sure that you find the right one. That can be a daunting task at first, but I am here to walk you through the process and make it a bit easier on you. The most important thing is that you are finding the care you need.

Where Do I Even Start?

When you have experienced childhood trauma, it can be overwhelming to tackle. However, it is important that you take this step. Trauma experienced in childhood is not an isolated incident. It can cause many problems in your adult life, from your mental health to your physical wellness. Finding the right therapist can provide some relief for what you are experiencing.

So, let's create a game plan for you to find the help that you require. The first step is to find a therapist that you feel safe opening up to. There are different things to consider when looking for a therapist, but some of them include:

- Specialties (do they specialize in childhood trauma?)
- Gender (perhaps you feel more comfortable with a certain gender)

- Price (you want to remain within budget)
- Connection (you want someone you "click" with)

Once you have an idea of what you are looking for, there are various avenues you can take to find just the right therapist for you. A great tool to use is actually *Psychology Today's* website. They have a therapist finder where you can plug in your needs and find therapists that fit your criteria. You can ask for a therapist of a certain gender or one who specializes in different types of therapies. Furthermore, if you want a therapist that incorporates art therapy (something that I would personally recommend for this type of work), they have that as a criterion as well.

Furthermore, there are many local resources that you can seek out. Most cities have local health departments with resources for those who are seeking out therapy. They are incredibly budget-conscious and can send you in the right direction without breaking your budget. Their main goal is to see you happier and healthier. Seek out their contact information and look into the resources available to you. You might even be able to find a therapist who works on a sliding scale, or one who works with your insurance.

Don't forget to read reviews! We live in a digital age, and most therapists have an online presence where people can read and leave reviews about their experiences. These can be tantamount in making your decision. If you see that a therapist you are considering sucks at scheduling or follow-up, can that idea and move on to the next candidate.

I have full confidence that with these tools in your toolbelt, you will be able to find the right therapist for you. It might take some time. If you go to see someone and it doesn't feel like the right fit, don't be afraid to fire them! Move onto someone who is a better fit. Therapists aren't one-size-fits-all, and you do not need to feel beholden to the first therapist you visit.

Once you have found the right therapist for you, don't be afraid to jump in the deep end. They are there to guide you through the messiness of your childhood wounds. Don't hold back when discussing them. They need all of the information you can give them to truly help you. I understand it can be hard to open up to a perfect stranger, so if you need some time to acclimate, don't view that as a failure. This is all new! You have the right to take your time.

THE BOTTOM LINE

Identifying and healing childhood wounds can be a practice in patience and self-love. Though it may feel foreign, you have all the tools available to you. You just need to implement them. I believe that you can move on past these wounds and start working on a brighter future.

Thus far, we have discussed how to diagnose the wounds that were inflicted on our inner child and how to find them within yourself. The next chapter will focus on how to allow them to run free. You want to keep up the momentum, so keep reading!

5

CREATING AN INVITING SPACE— A PATH TO HEALING

DOES IT REALLY NEED MY PERMISSION?

There are some that might be asking, "Does this inner child really need my say-so to make themselves known?" The answer is: Well, kind of. If your inner child is currently shoved down deep and is not coming out to play, it might be because it was taught that coming out was not safe. It is up to you to remind that part of yourself that you are safe. It is okay to come out into the light of day.

As adults, there may be many reasons our inner child feels unsafe coming out into the open. For instance, maybe you find the idea of letting out that playfulness to be irresponsible. Perhaps someone has made you feel like you cannot express that part of yourself. The possibilities are near endless, but the solution is simple.

Invite your inner child to a safe environment. We've gone over how to identify wounds and heal our inner child, but now comes the fun part: inviting it to come play. This can be a harder process for some than others. That might mean your inner child is buried under layers of responsibilities and trauma.

The first step in this process is to stop numbing your feelings. Children often don't bother to try hiding or dampening their emotions. They wear their heart on their sleeve. As an adult, we've tempered that somewhat, but it's important that we still allow ourselves to feel what we need to feel.

This can lead down a slippery slope where we actively avoid our feelings through things like vegging in front of the TV to more extreme measures like numbing with alcohol. Running away from emotions you are feeling is not just harmful to your inner child, it is also damaging your life as a whole. It can be a scary process to open oneself up after being closed off for so long, but put down the remote or the bottle. It is time to sit with your feelings and learn what they are trying to tell you.

Furthermore, don't try to rush the process. Children are easily spooked, and the same is true of your inner child. Moving too fast or with too much urgency can set you back. Move forward with slow but deliberate intent. Coax the inner child out as though you were speaking to a young child. In a sense, you are.

Once doors start opening and you start feeling more connected to that spirit within you, you can pick up the pace. However, the early steps should be taken with the utmost of care. Don't put too much pressure on yourself to be a new person by Tuesday. This is a delicate process and takes time.

That is not to say that you shouldn't be giving this all you have, however. In fact, I want you to throw a lot of your inhibitions out the window. Whenever you think, "Well, that just seems absurd," stop and ask yourself why. Is it really absurd, or are you holding yourself back? You want to have the fearlessness of a child to reawaken that child.

Once you set the groundwork for creating a safe environment for your inner child, the fun part begins. Your spirit has awakened to new prospects. Pursue passions and laughter consciously! That's right, whatever lights a spark in your soul and puts a twinkle in your eye, chase after it. Whether that be reading fantasy novels or doing your own artwork, pursue the things that once made you excited about life.

Now that your inner child knows that it is safe to show themselves, you will find this coming easier to you than it did in the past. You can explore that which brings you to life, and an added bonus will be that your inner child will begin to awaken more and more. This will help you heal old wounds and get a boost of self-confidence, along with many other benefits already noted in this book.

MEET AND CONNECT

Once you have established a safe place for your inner child, you will want to begin connecting with it. This might sound strange, but it's a great idea to try starting a dialogue with that part of yourself. Remember, this is your inner child, so approach with a gentle spirit. Converse with them as you would a real-life child; gently and with understanding. Have compassion for that inner child and everything they have gone through throughout your lifetime

There are several ways you can converse and connect with your inner child, but let's go through some of the basic ideas. Don't be afraid to try out something that seems silly or makes you uncomfortable. This entire process can be a bit silly and uncomfortable at times, but it pays itself back in spades.

First off, formulate a dialogue. Converse with this inner child. Talk to the child that you were and the child that still resides somewhere in your consciousness. They have been waiting to speak with you. Tell them loving and nurturing things. "I love you." "I'm sorry that happened." "You are okay now." All of these statements need to be said. If you're not keen on saying this out loud, that's okay. I've got you covered.

You can also write a letter to your younger self. Try to remember what you went through as a child—good and bad—and meet that child where they "are." This could mean meeting them in their joy or in their hurt. Don't shy away from either. Write a letter with nurturing and compassionate statements to let your inner child know you appreciate them and what they did/do for you.

If it is hard to muster up any dialogue, written or otherwise, try taking a creative approach. Some of us are highly visual in nature, so use that to your advantage. Look at old pictures of yourself as a child and try to remember being them. Remember their hopes and their dreams, their fears and needs. Bring yourself back into that time in your life and reach out across the years to the you that once was. You might find they are more amenable to come out once you have progressed through this journey.

Try again once you have gone through a little more of this book. If I have done my job right, then you will find it to be a simpler process. As you become more comfortable, you'll find the line of communication takes less effort. That means you are on the right path. So, return to this a few times to do a bit of a "spot check," if you will.

For now, though, make sure that you do not try to force the issue. Simply open yourself up to the conversation and see what happens. You might surprise yourself. The inner child can be a bit of a chatterbox once they are finally given the chance to speak. So, be prepared for whatever comes. It could be an interesting conversation.

The bottom line is that you need to meet that inner child where they are and where they were. It sounds complicated, but it's a simple case of approaching your own inner light as though it *were* that child. Coax it out slowly and carefully and you'll find that they are bursting at the seams to come out.

ENGAGING CONVERSATIONS—SPEAK THE LINGO YOU FANCY

The thing about the inner child is, that at its core, it behaves as a child. While this is something we are hoping to harness and use for our day to day life, it can also get us into trouble when we speak too much from that place. It's all a matter of language. Your inner child is trying to say something and you just need to find the right words to guide you to what that child needs in the moment.

For instance, "Why was that person so mean to me?" or "I want a present. Where is *my* present?" We may feel these things and that is the inner child wanting to be heard and actually *listened* to. What you need to do is understand what that inner child is wanting and find a way to reparent them, in a way.

For instance, try using some of these phrases when dealing with your inner child and see if they feel right:

- We are kind to each other.
- It is not our job to make others happy.
- I see you and I hear you. I understand what it's like to feel sadness when disappointment happens. You are not alone.
- How much I love you is not conditional on how hard you work to make me happy.
- Our needs come before the needs of others.
- We eat when we are hungry.

Just these simple statements—and many more—can help you reparent and tone down the emotional turmoil your inner child might be feeling at times. It is imperative that you notice and recognize what emotions you are feeling. Then, speak kindly to yourself about those emotions.

On a somewhat related note, to be a fully realized person, you will want to work on regulating. Children are not terribly great at emotional regulation, so when you first open that door, you might feel a flood of emotions. That is normal, but you need the tools to harness those emotions for your benefit instead of getting lost in the storm of them.

Set time aside to process the complicated emotions you might be feeling and try to unravel them a little. Are you feeling frustrated? Sad? Angry? Name the emotion and trace back to what is causing it. It would look something like this:

"I am angry. Why am I angry?" Then, take some time to sit with that emotion and trace it back to its source. You might find that you are angry because your contributions are not appreciated at work, or your partner didn't do the dishes when you asked them to. The same can work with happy emotions, and it's a great practice to do this with the positive emotions, as well. "I am happy. Why am I happy? My friend's party is coming up and I am excited to participate!" Understanding where your emotions are coming from, whether negative or positive, is a useful skill that can help you learn to regulate those emotions. We are, after all, just kids who have grown up and become a bit more complex. Break down those complicated feelings and bring them to square one. You might be surprised at how easily regulation comes when you are more in tune with your emotions. The inner child can help you with that, with a little reparenting.

Your inner child is desperate for something. It might be validation, it might be attention, and it might even be a bit of release. When you practice engaging with them and with your own emotions, you will start to realize that understanding that inner child comes more easily to you. Listen, learn, and move forward in your journey.

THE BOTTOM LINE

Communicating with your inner child effectively is key to inviting them out to play. You need to understand how to make them feel safe in the environment around you and speak their language. With the proper care, you can meet and connect with your inner child in a meaningful way.

Your inner child wants to feel seen and heard, so give them that. Get to the bottom of their emotions that are coming through. Reparent them on how to handle those complex feelings. If you practice engaging with your own emotions, it will be easier to engage with the emotions of your inner child.

Practice this, continue to communicate, and watch your relationship with your inner child flourish.

6

WHAT IF I WAS NOT
PARTICULARLY TRAUMATIZED?

A question you might be asking as you go through this book is, "Well, what if I lived a fairly charmed childhood?" If you did not face a lot of trauma growing up, you might feel a bit left out of the conversation about healing your inner child. However, this book and these practices are still for you. They will just look a little different.

Don't feel shame for having a great childhood. It's a beautiful thing. You don't need to carry the burden of those who have lived through trauma. You received a beautiful blessing and walking through these steps might actually be a lot easier for you than others. Rejoice in that and move forward.

A SWEET CHILDHOOD IS WORTH RELIVING

So, you lived a childhood free of trauma and actually remember it with fondness. That's great! That does not mean that you do not need to reconnect with your inner child. It just means that the process might be a little easier for you. It will still be beneficial in the long run for you to uncover that inner spark that might have been dampened by the responsibilities of being an adult.

First of all, let me say that I am truly glad you experienced a blessed childhood. There are many who cannot say the same, and it always brings me joy to hear about those who were not scarred by their formative years. It gives me hope to know that there are people out there untouched by trauma.

For you, it is still important to revisit your childhood and revel in the memories. Though you might not have wounds to heal, you still have things you can learn from that time in your life. Revisiting your childhood can uncover things that remind you what it was like to be a child. It will reignite that childlike spark within you and set you on the right course.

So, what about your childhood was so great? That's up to you to discover. I have met people from all types of backgrounds and walks of life who express joy at the memory of their childhood. It is interesting to see that all of these vastly different people have a shared experience, and there is a reason for that. There is no one formula for a happy childhood. It can look different from person to person.

Walk through memory lane and revisit the things that brought you to life and that sparked a light in your life. There are many you can revisit. Here are some great ideas that might spark something:

- Christmas morning with your family
- Your first big crush and that butterfly feeling
- Hearing the sound of the ice cream truck going by
- Learning to ride your bike
- Climbing a tree
- School dismissals due to snow
- Blowing out the candles on your birthday cake
- Enjoying arts and crafts

It may have been a while since you have dug up these memories. If you struggle to recall those feelings, it might be time to bust out old pictures and take a walk down memory lane. You might surprise yourself with the emotions that arise as you revisit these beautiful memories.

Your inner child remembers all of these memories with utter clarity. After all, they were there for all of them. When you delve into these moments, you might feel a stirring within you—something like excitement or exhilaration. That's great! It means your inner child is waking from their slumber and coming out to play. These memories are like strings through the labyrinth for that child to reconnect with you.

Once you have reconnected with these memories, let your heart well up with gratitude. It's an important part of the process to allow yourself a moment of gratitude for the childhood that you had, safe from trauma. This feeling can bring you closer to your inner child and all they have to offer you with their presence.

Don't let that gratitude die out. Return to those memories often if you must, but keeping your heart in a place of gratitude allows you to live in a place of contentment. You might find yourself walking through life feeling lighter and more carefree.

Understanding that you have lived a blessed life is not something to feel ashamed of. Just because others have suffered does not mean you should pay penance by denying the blessings of your childhood.

BE THE SALT OF THE EARTH

You had a childhood that was blessed within a family that was not dysfunctional. This is a true blessing in this world. Now that you have taken a trip down memory lane and identified that which made it special, it's time to take that and turn it into action. Should you choose to have children, this is especially important. Passing down a wonderful childhood to your children is one of the most concrete ways of which you can do this.

If you choose to have children, make sure that you remember what made your childhood so beautiful, and create that same environment for them. Be the parent that you were lucky enough to have. Create those same blissful memories for your little one. Prepare them for a world that will do its best to steal their spark.

This can seem like a daunting task when you look at the state of the world right now. It's a scary place, with the news cycle reminding you of everything you should be fearing. In a world like this, it can seem like an impossible task to provide a space where your children can feel safe. However, it is ultimately in your hands to provide this for them.

Traumatic events are happening everywhere, leaving us scared for the future. However, if you are a parent, you have it within you to help build a better future. What we need right now is not more fear. We need the next generation equipped for the world which they will inherit. Children who have been brought up to be fulfilled and empathetic adults can ultimately change the face of the world.

If you are feeling discouraged about the state of the world, that is completely understandable. We have all watched the news recently in shock and horror at the evil that exists out there. However, maintain hope that this next generation will be the one to break the cycle. Do the hard work and watch your child flourish within their environment, ready to take on the world.

Maybe you have chosen not to have kids or do not currently have any. That is okay. It is still possible to share that "salt of the earth" energy with those around you. This can look like volunteering at a shelter or sharing your wisdom with nieces and nephews. This can look like a lot of things, but it is up to you to share your love and compassion with those around you, even if it's just your partner or a friend.

EMBRACING THE HEALTHY INNER CHILD

When your inner child has found some ground in your current life, it means you have a healthy relationship with it—congrats! Though the challenge might not have been as intense as those for which childhood was traumatic, it is still a laudable achievement worth celebrating. Having a healthy inner child can really open up doors to a more fulfilling life. Rather than sleepwalking through a dull existence, you are awake to the wonders of the world, and I commend you on reaching this part of your journey.

If you had a happy and fulfilling childhood, embrace it and revel in your healthy inner child. You are among the fortunate who have few wounds to address, and that means opening up your inner child can be fruitful without stirring up painful memories of the past. I wish you the best in your continuing journey.

While we are discussing the matter of having a healthy inner child, it's important to note the benefits of this. There are many, and they make life all the more interesting. There are too many to address here, but let's touch on a few of the most important.

You Are Curious

There is an old adage, "curiosity killed the cat," but what most people don't know is that the latter half of this adage is, "but satisfaction brought it back." Curiosity is not something to shy away from. There is much to marvel at in this world, and embracing that curiosity of a child can give you a newfound appreciation for it.

Kids love to learn and are naturally inquisitive. With a healthy inner child, you might find that you have a thirst for knowledge. This unquenchable thirst is an asset in so many ways. Not only does it open you up to fully appreciate the wonders of the world, it can provide a fantastic leg-up in your everyday pursuits, be it the job market or passion projects.

That curiosity will only grow as you continue to seek out your inner child and become more connected with them. There is a great big world out there and there is so much to explore and discover, so start healing that inner child and viewing the world through curious eyes. You won't regret it.

You Make Small Things Enjoyable

Kids are fantastic at finding the joy in small things. Just running errands with their parents can be a fantastic day for them. Maybe along the way you lost a bit of that exuberance, but now that you are connecting with your inner child, it's coming back. A trip to the grocery store is now an adventure and a chance to treat yourself. A cup of coffee is not so much a necessary part of your day, but a time when you can revel in the flavor and aroma of your favorite morning drink.

Adults who have a healthy inner child will find small, everyday things much more enjoyable than they would have imagined. Lean into this. Instead of resigning yourself to monotony, you have found a way to make every day a new and exciting experience.

You might not realize it, but this can be the key to happiness in everyday life. When you start looking at everything with eyes of curiosity and wonder, you will realize that you have a newfound joy. So make your errands an adventure. Reward yourself for paying your bills on time. Find ways to enjoy the small things.

You Persevere

Let's talk about perseverance and resilience again. We discussed it earlier in this book when talking about the baby learning to walk. This might seem like an infantilizing comparison, so let's look at it through the eyes of a slightly older child. When a kid decides they want to ride a bike, they go all out. They shake off the cuts and bruises of their fall and get right back on that bike.

Someone with a healthy inner child has that same kind of perseverance. They do not give up at the first sign of trouble. They shake the dust off and continue on their way, intent on their objective. That's commendable, and is also a sure sign that you are on the right path.

Your innate strength that comes from that inner child will serve you well as you move through your everyday life. You will learn to roll with the punches and discover a new way of thinking. You won't view temporary setbacks as the end of the journey, but as an opportunity to find a new path. Thank your inner child for the strength they have granted you to be able to persevere in the face of difficulties.

You Stay Active

Children do not need to be told to exercise. They are constantly on the go: running, climbing trees, and swimming in the neighborhood pool. They revel in the ability to push themselves and stay active.

This may be something that a lot of adults have lost along the way. Getting home from work exhausted, the last thing they want to do is get up and do something active. The day has taken a toll on them. However, with a healthy inner child, this instinct to remain active comes more naturally. They know the world is their playground and they revel in the opportunity to stay active and on the go.

For many, this takes the form of participating in enjoyable workout classes such as Zumba or dance classes. For others, this might mean they break out that old bike that has been collecting dust in the attic. Whatever it looks like, those with a healthy inner child understand the benefit of staying active and feel the desire to do so.

You Are More Optimistic

Children are oftentimes just little rays of sunshine. They have yet to be embittered by the world, and so see it in its most positive light. They marvel at Christmas lights and just *know* they will be picked to play on the basketball team. Even disappointment barely slows them down as they continue to believe in a world where good things happen. They are not yet jaded, and thus have the ability to see the world in a light that a lot of us are lacking.

Someone with a healthy inner child will see signs of this develop in their life. Gone is the trademark cynicism of adulthood. Instead, you choose to see the world as full of opportunities. You have shed the jaded exterior that you have been carrying around and now see the world anew through the eyes of a child. This is not only good for your own mental well-being, but also for the world in general. We need more people in this world who can see the light. We need more people who choose to pursue it.

You See the Beauty in Nature

This one might take you by surprise. Children take the time to smell the proverbial *and* literal roses. They marvel at nature's wonder, and enjoy all that it has to offer. They climb trees, pick weeds as though they were flowers, and collect cool rocks they find on a walk. They don't need to be told the world is an incredible place; they see it whenever they step outside.

As your inner child begins to awaken, you might start to realize that your love for nature has also reawakened. You take time to admire the flowers growing in the cracks of the concrete on the way to work. You spend time drinking coffee as you watch the sunrise. Suddenly, the world has taken on a new wonder for you. That is a great sign of healing and growth for your inner child.

So go for a hike in the woods or spend some time in your garden. Continue to marvel at the wonder of nature. It will only nurture your inner child and give it the chance to grow further. Those walks and that gardening might seem like small things, but in fact, they are a big step in your journey.

You Are Adaptable

Think about it for a moment. Children deal with constant change, whether it's changing schools, moving with their family, or even just the development of their own body and consciousness. They understand what it is to roll with change, because they do not really have much of a choice. This adaptability suits them well and serves them as they move through life.

Somewhere along the way, adults lost that sense of adaptability. The slightest change in a scheduled meeting at work can send them into a frazzled state. However, with a fully realized inner child, people are more able to roll with the punches. They see things for what they are and learn how to be fluid with their time and energy.

This skill is of utmost importance in an ever-changing world. When you have the spirit of an adaptable child, you are able to deal with a variety of situations. You think on your feet and can deal with whatever life throws at you. This kind of attitude and spirit serves you well in everything, from interpersonal relationships to the workplace.

You Don't Care What Other People Think of You

Children are truly oblivious to the opinions of others. They do their own thing and don't spend much time worrying about how it will be received. They are unabashedly themselves at all time, with no shame or self-consciousness. They are truly comfortable in their skin and don't care who knows it.

Over time, this attitude has probably eroded in a lot of us. Suddenly, we're worried about what Becky in accounting thought about how we said good morning. We're worried our friends won't like our new haircut (even though we love it). Every step we take, we let others be party to our decisions.

With an awakened inner child, we are able to shed some of that responsibility. You still care about the *feelings* of others. You aren't unempathetic. It is just that you no longer feel like you need the permission of others to do your own thing. You feel free to be yourself without worrying about what others might think of your actions. It's a beautiful and freeing feeling. Appreciate it and revel in it.

You Dream Big

Probably my favorite thing about children is that they are not afraid to dream big. They aren't afraid to reach for the stars, comfortable in knowing that failure isn't world ending. Ask any group of children what they want to be when they get older and you'll get a variety of answers like "an actress," "a writer," or "an artist." They don't know what it's like to dream small. They know what they want and they pursue it with a wild abandon.

Over time, life has chipped away at that spirit in many of us. We begin to accept life as it is, never attempting to think outside of the box. However, with your connection with that inner child, you may have noticed that you are beginning to dream big again. Sure, maybe you no longer want to play for the NBA, but you have stopped putting arbitrary limits on your dreams.

This is a great place to be; a wonderful place. Brush off that old manuscript you haven't touched in a while. Start practicing your art skills. Maybe you won't be James Patterson or Banksy, but you no longer need to hold yourself back when it comes to reaching for the stars. Go out and get what you want, because your dreaming spirit is finally waking up.

You Are Kind to Others

Let's be honest. Children know how to love much better than we as adults do. Their love is absolute, with no conditions. They make friends quickly and easily. All it takes is a shared love for The Wiggles and a couple of juice boxes and they have a new best friend. They talk to strangers on the street to compliment them on their pretty hair. They are *kind*.

The frustrations of daily life can sometimes sap this kindness out of us. Don't fault yourself for this if you have gone through it. The world is a taxing place at times, and we sometimes lose touch with that kind spirit. However, as our inner child evolves, we might notice that we are slower to frustrate and quicker to understand others. We extend kindness more easily and freely.

This kindness is not just reserved for others, either. You might find that you are gentler and kinder with *yourself*, something that may not have come easy at first. This inner child is taking your hand and showing you how to greet the world with kindness and a full heart.

THE BOTTOM LINE

These admirable traits that you have learned from your inner child may not make your life *easier*, but they will definitely make it more enjoyable. Troubles will still come, but you will have new tools with which to approach these problems. Take joy in this newly discovered relationship with your inner child and face the day with newfound confidence.

This might sound trite, but it really is the better way to walk through life. Seeing the world through the eyes of your inner child may not only help you get further in your life, but it gives you a reason for living it. It brings with it a newfound joy and admiration for the world around you.

Once you have found that inner child, you will want to learn how to navigate life with this new lens. The next chapter will cover how to reconcile the child with the adult in you. It may sound like a complicated process, but I will lead you through every step.

7

MERGING THE CHILD WITH THE ADULT

So, now what? You've rediscovered your inner child and you are reaping the benefits. That should be it, right? Well, it is a bit more complex than that. You need to find a way to merge that childlike spirit with the existing adult that you are. The two can actually coexist rather harmoniously. You just need the right ideas and tools to aid you in this process of convergence.

WHO IS THE ADULT?

The adult in this equation is you, as you are now. The experiences you have been through and the responsibilities you have taken upon yourself have created the adult you are today. Every choice you have made has led you to this point.

The adult in this equation is the one who has to handle the day-to-day. You have to go to work, pay the bills, and maintain your relationships. This is not something you can fully depend upon your inner child for. Though they may provide you confidence and needed self-esteem to excel in these areas, it is still up to the "inner adult" to take care of business.

This "inner adult" is not the enemy. Though you may feel like that's where this book has been headed, it's in fact a good thing that you have grown and developed. There is no shame in leaning on that inner adult to get things done. As noted before, children tend to be highly distractible. They aren't necessarily the best part of your consciousness to rely upon when negotiating for a new salary, though the confidence they provide could definitely help.

Getting in touch with your inner child is a good thing. It opens you up to a world of wonder, rather than the hum-drum day-to-day. However, they shouldn't be the one driving the car all the time. Children, while amazing, are also incredibly reactionary and have a hard time regulating.

In these instances, you want to step in and "parent" your inner child. You need to make sure that their needs are being met while you are still tending to what needs tending. The inner adult still needs to be honored as a part of who we are. It might not be the most 'fun' part of ourselves, but it is what keeps us in balance. Sometimes that inner adult needs to do some reparenting of the inner child. We've discussed this at a surface level when it came to providing a safe place for the inner child. However, it goes deeper than that.

Parenting your inner child needs to be somewhat of a balance. The inner adult needs to ultimately be in control, but they also need to allow the inner child to express themselves. This fine balance can seem difficult, but it is actually quite simple. Think of it in terms of an actual parent-child relationship.

The adult is the one that accepts the child for who they are and loves them for it. However, *because* they love them, they do not allow them to make all of the decisions. They know that the child is incapable of the responsibility. So, no, no ice cream for dinner every night. No telling off your boss because he's being a real stinkin' jerk. Rein in those impulses and teach your inner child when it is okay to roam free, and when you need to be at the wheel.

Furthermore, your childlike self has weaknesses when they are at the reins too often. It can lead to a mentality of victimhood and helplessness. Children don't often feel in control, and when you view your entire life through that lens, it can start to become overwhelming.

Getting in touch with your inner child is great, but it's also important to remember the responsibilities you have as an adult. Parenting your inner child can be taxing at times, especially when they have suffered wounds from childhood. However, with the right balance between adult and child, you can flourish in your day-to-day.

WHO IS THE CHILD?

The child, as we have noted, is considered your true essence. The 'you' that entered this world. You were not a blank slate when you came to be. You were born with innate traits—strengths and weaknesses. However, when we break it down, what does that really mean in reference to the adult we are now?

In essence, the inner child is the part of you that was there in the beginning. The one that experienced your childhood and all the highs and lows that came with it. Your inner child is that inner spark that tells you to marvel at the world around you. It's what tells you to slow down and have a little fun from time to time. It is an important part of who you are, which is why you are seeking out a way to connect with it. However, it's important to address who the inner child is in relation to the adult that you are now.

Your inner child isn't all there is to you. In fact, it isn't even all the *good* that is in you. There are many great traits and strengths you have picked up as an adult that serve you well. For instance, you no longer have a problem with tantrums that send you to timeout. (Or, at least, I hope not.) You have learned to regulate and temper your reactions.

Still, the child is there for when you need a breath of fresh air—a moment to step out of the dull routine of adulthood. They are there for you when you just need to cuddle a plushie and color in one of those awesome coloring books. They are there for you when you need resilience or an optimistic outlook.

Inner children are there to be protected and are there to protect. Allow me to explain. We want to protect our inner child because they are the light that lives within us. The innate essence of who we are. They existed before any wounds; before any damage was done. They are to be protected, because in a way, they are like real children.

On the flip side, they are there to protect because of what they can offer us. Their kindness comes out when a situation is tense, to diffuse the situation. Their hope is there in our most desperate hour. We find them in the recesses of our mind when we are in a place where we need to think creatively.

I don't want you coming out of this chapter thinking that I am backtracking. The inner child is still an important part of you that is important to embrace. However, they also have a time and a place. Furthermore, parenting of that inner child might be necessary if there are wounds present that show up in your everyday life.

In the end, your inner child is something that is there to add some color to your life. They are there to teach you important lessons that you may have forgotten. However, they should not be at the wheel of your life at all times. Sometimes it is healthy to take a step back and do some heavy duty 'adulting.' This doesn't mean you are rejecting your inner child.

It means you are a healthy enough individual to recognize that a balance must be struck.

FIND THE ROOTS OF YOUR ADULT PROBLEMS

There is another benefit of opening yourself up to your inner child. It teaches you about yourself; you just have to be listening and paying attention. Your inner child can inform the decisions you make and the problems you have as an adult. Are you closed off? Do you struggle to find joy in hobbies like you used to? That's your inner child, wounded and calling out for your attention.

Though we are born with innate traits, we also pick up strengths and weaknesses with every experience we go through. If you notice that you have issues in your adult life, you can revisit your child self to figure out where that disconnect is. Perhaps it was a traumatic childhood. Maybe it was a lack of stability. It could even be a need that was never fully met when you were a child. Whatever the reason, your experiences are showing up in your adult life in the form of issues and bad habits.

That is why it is so important to heal the wounds inflicted on your inner child. By doing the work and really exploring your childhood, you can better understand what you are facing today. By healing wounds of the past, you can change your current experience. This is important to understand and remember.

If you are facing an inner child marred by the scars of trauma, it might be time to discuss your experiences with a licensed therapist. As mentioned in chapter four, sometimes the baggage is too heavy for us to unpack on our own. We need a trained professional to help us better understand these struggles we have faced. There is no shame in that. In fact, it is commendable to seek out the help that you need. So many are afraid to do so.

Maybe it was simply a desire or need that was never met. Maybe you were never able to express yourself as a child. This can go two ways: Either you are expressing yourself all over the place, or you have cut yourself off from communication. Healing the wound of feeling unheard can help you find a better balance to how you communicate with others and bolster better mental well-being in the long run.

Maybe you lost someone or something dear to you as a child; the death of a loved one or moving from your childhood home when you were too young to understand. You did not have the capacity to fully understand what was happening at the time, and therefore did not have the bandwidth to deal with it.

Whatever the cause of your adult issues, it is important to get to that root and really deal with it. Whether that means going to counseling or doing some good old soul searching, it is really up to you. I can't tell you what will be best for your inner child and your current state. However, it is important not to ignore these red flags. Instead, lean into the understanding of them, hoping to find relief on the other side.

HOW TO MERGE SAFELY

As mentioned before in this chapter, there needs to be a certain merging of your inner child and current adult self. This can seem complicated at first, but it's important to be a balanced individual. You want the best of both worlds, so let's dive into what that truly looks like.

The most important step in embracing and healing your inner child is to acknowledge that they exist. That's it! That's the first step. What happens when we open this door, however, is sometimes that the child self thinks they get to have free rein of our lives. This couldn't be further from the truth.

Though it is important to be in touch with that childlike spirit, you also want to remain realistic. You are an adult with responsibilities and people counting on you. You can't just up and quit your job to join the traveling circus, and you can't act like a child in your interpersonal relationships.

Yes, that is where a lot of the problems come in when doing inner child work. When that door gets opened, we get the good with the bad. Children are remarkable creatures full of wonder and excitement. However, they are also sometimes selfish and reactionary. This can spell disaster in interpersonal relationships.

It is important to set boundaries to keep your inner child from wreaking havoc. 'Boundaries' has become something of a buzz word in recent years, but its importance should not be belittled. Boundaries keep us safe and respected. It might sound strange to set boundaries with ourselves, but I promise you that you might be the most important person to set boundaries with.

Make sure you designate when the inner child is allowed to take the reins. It should not be in a meeting with your boss or an argument with your significant other. That is when you need to set boundaries. Tell your inner child, "I hear you and I understand what you are feeling, but it's adult time right now." Setting that boundary with your inner child might seem weird at first, but with practice, you can find an even balance.

Once you have these boundaries in place, you will find that you are a much happier and more productive person. You have harnessed the ability to view the world as a child while maneuvering the world as an adult. It truly is the best of both worlds, and something that is worth pursuing.

Once you have merged these two sides of yourself, you will find that they are not at war with each other. In fact, they complement each other well. Once you are able to walk the line between the two, you will find that doors will open to you in ways that they haven't before. You will find that you get to enjoy the joys of childhood while also maintaining a healthy adult life, which is really what we all want, right?

You are your best advocate. Whatever you need to make this happen, make sure it happens. If that means talking to a trained professional, so be it. If it means walking down memory lane and better understanding the experiences that you couldn't grasp as a child, do that. Your future is in your hands, and it will be a much brighter one—once you are able to find your balance.

THE BOTTOM LINE

Though it might not seem like it at times, there is a clear distinction to the inner child and your inner adult. Both are necessary to your survival and happiness. Both deserve equal seats at the table. They just do not belong at the *same* seat. Understanding how both roles interplay is an important step in understanding how to make them cooperate with each other.

The adult should be the one in the driver's seat most of the time. When you're in a board meeting or deciding what to do with your paycheck, you might want to make sure they're at the helm. Not to say that the inner child does not get *some* say in what happens, but the decisions should be made by the adult, as would happen in a parenting relationship.

After all, that is a bit of what you're doing—reparenting the child within.

8

THE INNER CHILD IN THOSE
YOU LOVE

While you are on this journey, you are not alone. This can be comforting and frustrating, all at the same time. You might not realize this now, but there might even be people in your own life who are reading this very book, or one similar to it. It is a common practice in today's world to reconnect with that lost inner child.

You need to understand this with a sense of compassion and truly live it. Walk the walk, so to speak. Have patience with those around you who are also rediscovering their inner child. Understand that they might be tackling some heavy stuff in order to heal themselves.

YOUR NON-JUDGMENTAL GROWNUP SELF

Judgment is the enemy of personal progress. When you judge others and their particular journey to discover their inner child, you are not only harming them, you are harming your own personal growth. Everyone's journey will look a little different, and it benefits no one to make critical observations of others.

The fact of the matter is, this will become less of a problem as you continue to connect with your inner child. Children are remarkably nonjudgmental. However, when the adult is at the wheel, we might feel some resentment and criticism for those around us, especially those on the same journey, taking a different path.

Stop that. Really, just stop it. There is no good in criticizing the journey of others. As adults, we often become cynical and critical of others. It can be hard to shed that behavior, but I am here to walk you through the steps it will take to be a happier and less judgmental person.

Start by identifying your motivation for judging. That is always where you need to start when correcting a problem—identifying the root of it.

There might be a good reason you are judging another person. However, the impetus for judgment is often to compare ourselves to the other person to make ourselves feel better about our own journey.

The comparison game is dangerous and should be avoided at all costs. It can leave us feeling resentful and possibly holier-than-thou. You don't want to be that person. If you have legitimate criticism of someone, it is best to either tell them in a constructive fashion or to let it go. Coming at it from any other place than compassion can often lead to more harm. If you are playing the comparison game, though, it is best to abandon the judgment altogether.

Once you have identified the root of your judgment, it is best to look inward once again and identify your own imperfections. That might sound counterintuitive, but there is a reason that this is step two. Yes, that person might not be doing things the way you think they should be done. However, it is important to acknowledge that you have your own shortcomings and might not be doing everything right either.

When you admit to yourself that you are not perfect (no one is), then you can relinquish that need to judge others. As an added bonus, it takes a bit of pressure off your shoulders. You don't have to be the judge and jury of others. You are just as flawed as they are, and therefore don't need to shoulder that responsibility.

Next, you need to understand that you are not them. Let me explain further. We are all, on some level, a sum of our experiences. You have different experiences from that other person. You don't know the struggles and pain that they have seen. That pain informs their decisions. If you can understand that, you can begin to extend grace and relinquish that death grip you have on judgment.

We all have different struggles, and therefore should not be playing the comparison game at all. What might come easily to you could be extremely difficult for someone with different wounds. You might never have the full story of someone's pain, so judging their actions can leave you looking cold and uncaring.

Never assume that others take action without reason. Everyone has experiences that inform their decisions. Once you better understand that, you'll be in a better place to accept people without judging their actions.

Another thing to consider is how you feel when that judgment is directed at you. You might be able to recall with utter clarity the last time someone judged you. It didn't feel great, did it? Especially if that person was unaware of your personal struggles and the ins and outs of your life.

That pain of feeling judged should inform how you react to others. Do not spread the pain around by falling into the same patterns as those who judged and hurt you. It might feel better for a moment to compare yourself to someone else and feel like you are superior. However, in the long run, you are giving into negativity, specifically negativity that has no basis in reality and has caused you harm in the past.

Imagine for a moment judging someone and then discovering their life story. You might find yourself feeling awful for your earlier criticism. This ends up causing harm to both the person you are judging and your own personal growth. Guilt and shame are suppressors of the inner child, so avoid them at all cost. Don't give yourself a reason to feel ashamed of yourself.

However, this is not just about you. So far, I have walked you through the ways in which judgment can be harmful primarily to *you*. However, you are not the person being judged. Your judgment, even when not spoken aloud, can often be sensed by the other person. They might feel negatively about themselves following your assessment, and that is just a crummy thing to do to someone.

Everyone's journey will look a little different, so allow yourself and *others* grace. It is important to remember that as you go through this process. You are trying to reconnect to yourself from before you became judgmental. Allow that part of yourself to shine through and give others the benefit of the doubt.

STIFLE NOT!

Here's the thing. We have discussed the benefits for *you* exploring your inner child. However, you are not the only person on this planet. Others in your life will be undertaking this journey at some point or other, more than likely. That means that your spouse, child, friends, etc. might be taking up the call and pursuing their inner child. It is important that we discuss how to respond to this when it happens.

First and foremost, let them pursue this. Do not attempt to stifle their inner child, as that is not fair to them. It might be a transitional time for them and you both, but allow them that. It is only fair that you give them the same space that they gave you to explore your inner child.

This is not just a matter of fairness, though. It is a matter of love. If you want your loved one to truly experience life with wonder, then you need to allow them the space to find and embrace their inner child. With both of you taking this leap, you might find that your interpersonal relationship takes on a new shape. This can be a little scary, at first, not being used to it. Don't fear it; rather, embrace it.

This beautiful journey that you have undertaken shouldn't be hidden away. You should be sharing this wonderful process with your loved ones. After all, they have an inner child too, wanting to come out. It is not up to you whether they invite it out into the open or not. It is ultimately their decision, and is one you should respect.

Furthermore, a relationship truly blossoms when you allow the other person to be their true self. After all, relationships are all about honesty and vulnerability. When you stifle their inner child, you are shutting down that line of communication. This can lead to conflict or tension in the relationship—or worse—a total dissolution of it.

This is where the inner adult takes a little bit more of the lead. You need to understand the responsibility you have to this person. You care about them, you want them to be happy, and so you should allow them the space to discover that spark that might have dwindled over time.

We need a world where people have come to life. We need a world where people are in touch with their inner child. It would be pretty boring otherwise. Don't keep this beautiful process to yourself. Share with others and celebrate in their decision to embark on this journey. Resentment and judgment have no place in this work, so leave them at home.

CONNECTING ON A DEEPER LEVEL

Furthermore, you should appreciate the journey that they are undertaking. It can lead to a richer relationship with them. When someone has embraced their inner child, they are a more fully realized person. If you have both done the work, then you can enjoy a relationship of meaning and playfulness.

You might not understand their personal journey 100%, but you can appreciate the path that they are walking and build a better relationship from a place of understanding. This is exciting and meaningful. Throw away your judgment and resistance and reach out to your friend or family member with open arms. Do the work to create a healthy relationship

So, how does one do that? Relationships are complicated, and are often hard to really nurture. It can be especially difficult when both parties are involved with a journey that takes a lot out of them. However, there is a road map to deepening relationships that will greatly benefit you as you continue on this journey and they continue on theirs.

Practice Active Listening

You might have heard the term "active listening" and not really understood what it meant. After all, isn't listening inherently passive? However, this is not the case, and taking time to practice active listening can greatly impact your relationships—for the better!

Here's the thing. We as humans are not as great at communication as we would like to think. More to the point, we are not particularly talented at *really* listening. Active listening goes beyond hearing the other person; it is being an active participant in really listening to what they have to say.

It is vital that you begin working on active listening, as you will be better able to understand what the other person is trying to get across, both verbally and non-verbally. You want to ensure that you are truly getting to the heart of what they are saying. This can include repeating back to the other party what you thought you heard. You will often find that you are misunderstanding their point of view.

By doing this, you are allowing the other person to clear up any misunderstandings. You bypass the missed signals and hurt feelings and are able to focus on what really matters in the conversation. However, it's not all about repeating back to the other person. It also takes intense focus to really make sure you are actively listening.

You want to give complete attention to what the other person is saying and how they are saying it. So put away your phone and really listen to them. Furthermore, you want to make sure that you are asking questions, trying to get to the bottom of what they are really thinking and feeling.

Not only does this allow you to fully understand the other person, it makes them comfortable in your presence. They know that you are someone they can turn to when they need to talk something out. They know that they can share things with you and receive real acknowledgement in return. This is important when they have worked on their inner child, as inner children want nothing more than to feel seen and heard.

Respond sincerely. Instead of just waiting for your turn to talk, really take time to consider what the person is saying and respond with sincerity and insight. You will find that you have much more meaningful conversations when this is your everyday practice.

Set aside any motives that you might have. They have no place in active listening. You just want to hear out the other person and come to a place of understanding. For instance, sometimes someone wants to vent to you. They want empathy. However, you are already jumping ahead, trying to solve their problem. That might not be what they want or need in the moment, so pay attention to what they are actually saying. If you feel a solution is necessary, you can still provide them with one, but give them time to get what they need off their chest.

These exercises seem simple, but they might actually take some practice to get right; especially if you are not used to active listening. However, it is imperative to a healthy relationship that you start to understand these principles and implement them in your personal relationships.

Pay Attention to Feelings Behind Their Words

This one can be a bit more difficult than active listening as it takes some intuition and sometimes, some light probing. When you are listening to the other person, make sure you are paying attention to more than just *what* they are saying. Listen to *how* they are saying it as well. Is their tone resigned? Angry? Overwhelmed?

Being able to meet them on an emotional level is just as important as understanding what they are trying to say. Just as you met your inner child where they were, you must meet this person where *they* are. It can be difficult sometimes, as some people are difficult to read. In this case, there is no harm in asking the other person how they are feeling in the moment. They might even appreciate the check-in.

The best tip I can give you here is to get more comfortable with your own emotions so that you can better read and understand the emotions of others. You might start to notice that you can even pick up on others' emotions more easily, seeing through to the heart of the person with whom you are speaking. The more comfortable you are with your own emotions, the easier you'll be able to meet others on an emotional level.

Get Comfortable with Feedback (Giving and Receiving)

In order to have a deep and meaningful relationship, it is important that there is honesty. This can often come in the form of constructive feedback. There needs to be a give-and-take relationship here, with both parties feeling like they can express constructive criticism and also receive it without defensiveness.

Being frank and candid with one another might feel uncomfortable at first. However, staying in your comfort zone will keep your relationship stagnant. Growth demands unfettered but respectful honesty. With these conversations, you will notice that your relationship and your confidence within it begin new growth. This is because you now know where you stand with the other person, wholly.

Also make sure that you are admitting your mistakes and allowing the other person to respond with justified criticism. Nobody is perfect, the old adage goes, and it's true. By admitting your mistakes, you are opening yourself up to the other person and providing an example for them to do the same.

As uncomfortable as this might be, honesty and vulnerability are the foundation of a healthy relationship. If you want the most out of your relationship with others, you need to start getting comfortable with giving and receiving feedback.

Embracing Their Inner Child

Once you have built the foundation of a healthy relationship, it comes time to really begin to accept the other person's inner child. Get to know them. Learn how this experience has changed them. It might be like meeting a whole new person, and it might just be like meeting a new and improved version of the person you knew. Whatever the case, it's important that you make *their* inner child feel as comfortable as your own.

Maybe try doing some 'childish' activities together. Do a puzzle or go on a bike ride. Explore nature together. Finding ways to explore your inner children together can be a truly rewarding experience, and is one worth pursuing.

At the end of the day, you just want to make sure that you are making room for the other person to grow alongside you. There is a popular song, *Grow as We Go* by Ben Platt. I encourage you to give it a listen. Your growth should be a collaborative effort, not a competition or something to do solo, if you can help it. Reach out and explore this wonderful part of yourselves together.

THE BOTTOM LINE

The more you allow your partner to grow, the stronger your relationship becomes. Growing together is even better. It gives you a chance to get to know each other as you develop into better versions of yourselves. At the end of the day, your relationship should be built on trust and mutual respect. In order for that to happen, you must be willing to allow your partner this journey.

More often than not, their journey will look different than yours. Try not to judge it, as this just leads to hurt feelings and resentment. You want to encourage them, even if you do not quite understand the steps they are taking. As long as they are doing this in a healthy manner, it is not up for you to decide how they go about it.

Once you understand the inner child within you and others, you should have a better idea of how to take care of that spark you have. In case you are searching for ideas, however, the next chapter will cover self-care—and no, it won't just be about eating ice cream and lighting candles. Self-care is often misunderstood and so much more encompassing than we might imagine at first glance.

9

SELF-CARE PRACTICES FOR YOUR INNER CHILD

We've all heard the term "self-care." It's been a hot topic as of late, and sometimes the concept behind it can be a bit misconstrued. It's not all about chocolate bon bons and bubble baths. It is, well, taking care of one's self. This can include eating healthy and making sure you are getting exercise.

The same mentality goes for your inner child. You want to make sure that they are cared for; that their needs met. This chapter will focus on how you can best do that. It might not be what you are used to, but fear not, it is not a difficult practice. You just need to know what you are doing, going in.

BELIEVE: YOU DESERVE THIS

I joke that shame is often one of the first emotions we learn as children. It's like we're born and the word is immediately rubber-stamped on our fore-head. So, accepting that you deserve this healing experience can be a struggle. Even if you don't have a past that needs to be healed, you might be feeling shame about *that*. Shame comes so easily to us, so how do we stop this train in its tracks?

You need to start believing that you are worth this process. You are worth the healing and you are worth the fulfillment. Easier said than done, though, right? Well, there are practices you can implement to help your heart and mind to accept this new reality.

The fact of the matter is, this world thrives on shame. There's an entire beauty industry that wants us to feel ashamed of how we look. When we break it down, there is a lot of money in keeping us ashamed. That's no reason to allow the cycle to continue. Instead, say 'no' to shame and start living the life you deserve.

What's Holding You Back

Let's take a look at some of the reasons people feel they don't deserve to live a fulfilled life. By breaking down these individual ideas, we'll have a better understanding of where to go from here. If any of these resonate with you, I'm sorry, but we will walk through these difficult emotions together.

Past Sins

Perhaps the reason that you feel you do not deserve this type of self-kindness is because of mistakes you have made in your past. You feel as though your screw ups are unforgivable; or at the very least, undeserving of grace. These feelings are damaging, and frankly, wrong. You are not the worst thing you have ever done.

If you deal with this, you might feel as though your unhappiness is penance for the life which you have lived. However, we do not need more people carrying burdens out of a sense of paying penance. We need more people who have shed the shame and walked into a life where they are fully living.

Trauma

I have met many women who have experienced sexual trauma in their youth and have walked away from that experience feeling 'dirty.' No matter the trauma you may have experienced, there may be some residual shame surrounding it. Either you think that you somehow 'asked' for it to happen or that it has left you 'broken.' These are damaging beliefs, and as far from the truth as you can get.

Trauma is something that happened to you. This goes especially for childhood trauma. You had no say in what happened. It was done *to* you, and therefore you have nothing to feel ashamed of. This can be a difficult task and is something that you might need to unpack with a licensed therapist.

Whatever you went through, treat yourself with compassion and understand that your trauma does not define you as a human being. You are more than what happened to you. You are kind, you are loving, and you are strong. Do not forget that.

Critical Self-Image

Perhaps you just see yourself in a highly critical light. This can come from perfectionism, an excess of drive, or even a childhood where you were frequently criticized. Whatever the reason, you are unable to see yourself in a positive light. You have decided that happiness is based on who you are and you have fallen short of the mark. You are undeserving due to real or perceived shortcomings.

I don't think I have to say that this mentality is unhelpful to the journey on which you have embarked. You do not need to do or be anything 'special' to deserve love and care from yourself. You don't have to pass a test or clear the finishing line. It's a process open to all, even those who tend to be hard on themselves.

Walking into the Light

Okay, so we've covered what might be holding you back. Now, it is time to delve into how you start shedding those feelings of shame and walking into a healthier relationship with your inner child and proper self-care. It is worth the work. Depending on what is causing you to doubt this journey, your solution might look different from someone else's. These steps might not all relate to you, but pay attention to what does.

Making Amends

If you are dealing with feelings of shame and guilt for what you have done in the past, one of the best steps you can take is make amends with those that you have hurt. Give them a call or write them a letter. Even if you have lost contact with those you have hurt, writing a letter to them can be a great way to release that shame. You don't have to send it. Just having that 'conversation' can be healing.

If nothing else, that reconciliation written on paper can be a release of energy. That is what a lot of our emotions really boil down to—a type of energy. When you pour your heart out on the page, you can allow some of those repressed emotions about your past to release. You would be amazed at the doors this can open in your mind and heart.

Realize You Did the Best You Could at the Time

This can be an extremely difficult pill to swallow, but it is necessary to healing. You might not *feel* like you did the best you could, but remember, you were a child and operating on the knowledge that you had at the time. Whatever mistakes you might have made or hurt you might have caused was not due to malice. It was due to a lack of proper knowledge.

Even in your adult life this can apply. Oftentimes, we find ourselves holding ourselves accountable for mistakes that were just that—mistakes. Give yourself some leeway and grace. The world is a difficult place to navigate and we all stumble from time to time. You are not expected to be perfect, by any measure.

Resolve Your Trauma

When it comes to trauma, there really is no closing the book on it. It will always be a part of you in some way. However, you can work *through* the trauma, particularly by working with a licensed therapist who specializes in the field. You want to start looking at your trauma through a new lens and completely understand the intricacies of it to move forward.

It is important to note that working through trauma is a tough undertaking, and is not one to be taken lightly. Make sure that you are in a safe place in your life to start unpacking these old wounds. It is for your own well-being. However, the benefits might be just what you need.

Working through your trauma will not only allow you to accept self-compassion, it will help you move out of the shadows and into the light. This is necessary to not only connect to your inner child, but to help with your current situation. I encourage you to work through this and find the other side. It's beautiful here.

Directly Work on Your Self-Criticism

I know it is much easier to fall back on old habits and continue on the path of self-sabotage, but self-criticism needs to be looked at with, well, criticism. You think that when your brain tells you that you have done something wrong, the solution is to try harder. Instead, you need to retrain your brain.

What you might not realize is that it is less a cycle of failures than it is self-abuse. You tell yourself you're no good, you believe it, and then you behave as such. It is a pattern that does not serve you. A therapist friend once said to me, "The you inside of you hears what you are saying." That is to say, you internalize what you say to and about yourself, whether you think you do or not.

Try breaking this cycle by talking to yourself in a kinder way. There's a type of therapy called Radical Acceptance Therapy, and part of that process is learning how to diffuse your thoughts; to separate them from yourself and not let them label you. For instance, you might say to yourself, "I'm a slob." To diffuse that statement, you would say, "Sometimes, I can be messy." It stops becoming a defining statement and becomes something probably closer to the truth.

Self-compassion can be *extremely* hard when you are used to being so hyper-critical of yourself. Believe me, I know. I have walked this path. You might be shaking your head at this book right now and thinking that what I am saying doesn't apply to *you*. You really *are* terrible. However, I ask you to examine that for a moment and figure out what it is you think makes you so bad. More often than not, the people I help have a circular logic surrounding their own self-criticism and abuse.

Carry Forward Those Life Lessons

What all these reasons for not accepting the love and compassion toward yourself have in common are feeling stuck. You feel stuck in a moment or in a mindset. You feel as though you can't move forward and accept the happiness on the other side of this misery.

All of what I have mentioned in this chapter thus far can help break you out of that rut. However, there is a catchall for dealing with all of these issues, and that is behavioral changes. You want to see change? Then create change in your life.

This might look like volunteering at a battered women's shelter so you go from the mindset of victim to advocate. It might look like showing more love and compassion toward those around you. As you make these behavioral changes, you might start to realize that your mindset begins to change as well.

Carrying forward the lessons that life has taught you —the hard way or the easy way—can forever alter your course. Feeling stuck happens when you don't take direct action. So, pull yourself up off the floor and start taking care of yourself. Start showing love for others. You'll find your heart and mind open up along the way.

Understand Your Inherent Worth

As a human living on this planet you have inherent worth. You just do. We have all seen the viral video of the guy offering us a 20-dollar bill and then crumpling it and offering it to us again. The point here is that what happened to that bill did not corrupt its worth. We still want the 20 dollars, even if it's a little battered.

The same is true of humans. You are worth it because, well, you are. You were created by God or the Universe, whatever your spiritual belief may be, and you were put on this earth to really live. Living without self-compassion is a half-life I would not wish upon anyone. If you need to stand in front of the mirror and repeat some affirmations to yourself, do it! Alter your pattern of thinking and start realizing how amazing you really are. You have made it this far, after all.

You deserve happiness because you are a beautiful human who wants to do the hard work to better themselves. That right there is all the criteria you need to 'deserve' happiness and self-care. So, keep doing the work. Do not let your own lack of self-compassion keep you from living a full life.

THE DAILY PRACTICE

Now that we have gone over why you deserve self-care and self-compassion, let's dive into what that might look like day to day. I will give you some solid examples of how to practice good self-care for your inner child. Try them all out, if you are able, but choose what resonates best for you. After all, this is self-care, and you know yourself best. You will know what works for you.

When it comes to self-care for the inner child, it might look a little different than how we envision typical self-care. That's okay. This is all about trying new things; or rather, returning to some old things. Practicing self-care for your inner child can be tricky, but it can also be fun! So, loosen up and try some of these daily practices.

Journaling/Writing to Your Younger Self

I remember being a child and there was nothing more precious to me than my diary. I hid it away in a safe place and wrote down all of my deepest most personal thoughts. I have revisited it a few times and while there is definitely some superfluous stuff in there, I was also surprised at some of the wisdom that younger me had to share.

You might be out of practice when it comes to journaling, but try your hand at it. You do not have to write a manifesto for it to be worth doing. Just set aside five minutes every day to journal your thoughts. Maybe it's just what happened that day. Maybe it is something that has been on your mind a lot lately. Maybe it turns into creative free writing.

Whatever the case, journaling can bring you back into that mindset of being a child and let them voice what they need to.

Furthermore, it might be beneficial to write letters to your younger self. I know this might sound a little strange, but having that conversation with young you can be enlightening and healing. Tell them what they needed to hear back then: That they are enough, that they are appreciated, and that they are loved. Tell them what you wish you had known back then.

You might realize that this opens up some emotions within you. That's natural and okay. Let the emotions come, and let them teach you what they want to teach you. This is a healthy part of the process.

Do Things You Enjoyed as a Kid

In order to show your inner child that you appreciate them, do something that you used to enjoy as a child. This can be something small, like doing a puzzle, or something as elaborate as taking horseback lessons again. Whatever you can manage and think your inner child would enjoy, go do the thing!

The basis behind this is that you can remember the sweet things about childhood. Those early days of discovering new hobbies and exploring your interests were so much fun! Don't feel beholden to what are considered 'grown up' hobbies. If you want to bust out a coloring book, go for it! This is not about hobbies that can help you grow or enlighten you. It is about simply having fun.

I'm not necessarily telling you to go climb a tree (unless you feel so inclined), but leaning into those interests you had as a child can be so rewarding. Let loose and have some kid-friendly fun. There are a number of things you can try. Here's a list that might give you a place to start:

- Coloring books
- Crafting kits
- Riding your bike
- Reading books geared toward a younger audience
- Going swimming at the local pool (play mermaids!)
- Playing video games
- Playing sports
- Going for a long walk through the neighborhood at dusk

Notice that none of these are particularly refined or intellectual pursuits. This is by design. The purpose is not to grow intellectually, but to nourish your inner child. You might learn lessons far more important than any you can find in a dry, informative book.

Practice Compassionate Self-Talk

Look, we've gotten into a habit, as adults, of talking ourselves down. We forget our wallet at home and instinctively say, "Oh, I'm an idiot." First off, stop that. Secondly, start replacing that language with more compassionate talk toward yourself.

When speaking to yourself, stop and think for a moment if this would be an appropriate way for a parent to converse with a child. You obviously wouldn't call a child an idiot or stupid. So why are you speaking to yourself in such a negative way? Your inner child hears everything, and that negative self-talk is only making them further withdraw within you.

Instead, take a compassionate stance in your everyday struggles and talk to yourself compassionately and gently. Allow yourself to makes mistakes. Practice saying, "It's okay." Odds are, it is! Everyone makes mistakes, so this negative self-talk is not serving any purpose other than to make yourself feel awful.

This includes when you have been hurt or made to feel uncomfortable. Remind yourself that you are allowed to have those feelings. Say to yourself that you are allowed to feel how you feel and that these negative feelings will pass, just as you would a child. Don't belittle your own pain, but also do not let it have too much power over you.

Pet Animals

There is a reason there is such a thing as a therapy dog. You see it all the time at children's hospitals and colleges during finals weeks. There is something therapeutic about petting an animal. If you have pets at home, make sure you set some time aside for cuddles and love. It will be enjoyable for both of you and will bring you closer to your inner child.

If you don't have pets at home, consider occasionally stopping by the animal shelter in your area. They are always looking for volunteers to help walk dogs or socialize kittens. Stop in and see if they are looking for anyone. It doesn't have to be a daily thing, but you can stop by weekly to have a little time with some furry friends. The effects on your mood and your inner child will be immediately evident.

There is a reason that people have emotional support animals. They play an active role in our healing and our mental well-being. Having a pet or even taking time to play with animals at a shelter can be self-soothing, and can reactivate that part of your consciousness that holds your inner child.

Call Up a Childhood Friend

Sometimes, we just need a little reminder about what it means to be a child. Remember when we were kids and we'd have play dates with our friends? That might seem impractical now, but remember that FaceTime exists. Call up an old friend and have a quick video chat. However, make sure to keep the conversation light and childlike. No talk of politics or finances is allowed. Instead, talk about the exciting book you just read or the movie you can't wait to come out. Talk about your hobbies and your relationships. Tell jokes and laugh. Bring up memories from the "good old days."

This friend can be like a tether back to the you that once was. They knew you when you were a child, so there's no hiding from them. Also, your inner child will recognize them as a safe person and feel fine coming out to 'play.' Try to nourish this relationship and call often. Make it a regular thing so that you can both grow together.

This practice is great because you will fully remember the great parts of being a kid. When you chat, try to revisit old memories. Remember what it was like walking through the creek as a child, or playing video games until dawn at a sleepover. The more you open yourself up to this type of conversation, the more you will feel in tune with your childhood and all the blessings that you received from it.

Spend Some Time in Mindful Rest

The pace of today's world can be best categorized as go, go, go. We're always on the move, ready to tackle the next project, the next chore. However, sometimes, we need to take a moment and take a deep breath. Remind ourselves that we are not what we can accomplish in a day. I understand that you cannot always take the day off from 'adulting,' but you can take five to fifteen minutes of mindful rest to keep yourself connected to your innermost self.

Try meditation or a guided visualization to relax and embrace the peace of being at one with yourself. You merely need a few minutes to do this, and this rest can have a significant impact on your mental well-being and your ability to call your inner child out to play. Take a deep breath, ignore the to-do list for a few minutes, and simply *be*.

If meditation isn't your thing, put on some gentle music. I recommend using lofi as its purpose is to soothe. Take a few deep breaths and remain present in the moment. Remember how easy that was as a kid? We weren't worried about the next chore or tomorrow's work project. We were allowed to just *be*. Give yourself that space every day, for just a few minutes, and see the difference it makes.

THE BOTTOM LINE

The key to great self-care is believing you deserve it and taking the time for it. Once you have those beliefs down, you are on the road to success. Understand that this is not superfluous. Taking care of your mind is just as important as taking care of your body. So, while it is good to stay active and drink plenty of water, make sure that your mind is nourished, too. That means sometimes catering to your inner child. Get a little silly and embrace the silliness. You deserve to be happy. You deserve to be cared for—even by yourself.

While it can be easy to get caught in the guilt of taking time for yourself, it is absolutely vital to a fulfilling life. You want to be able to live a life that you don't have to escape from on a regular basis. Create the life around you that you dreamed of as a child. If you want to buy a plushie, buy the plushie. Who cares if you're 35? Remember, embracing the silliness is all part of the journey.

A SHORT MESSAGE FROM THE AUTHOR

Hey, are you enjoying the book? I'd love to hear your thoughts!

Many readers do not know how hard reviews are to come by, and how much they help an author.

I would be incredibly grateful if you could take just 60 seconds to write a brief review on Amazon, even if it's just a few sentences!

SCAN BELOW TO CREATE A REVIEW

Thank you for taking the time to share your thoughts!

Your review will genuinely make a difference for me and help gain exposure for my work.

Faye Mack

CONCLUSION

It is my hope that this book gave you clear guidance on how to invite your inner child out to play. I hope you feel more in tune with yourself and the world around you. Most of all, I hope you feel happier and more fulfilled. While this journey can be a difficult one, you are up to the task and I commend you on taking the very first steps.

When you are an adult, it is easy for your inner child to get lost in the fray. There is just too much demanding our adult attention. We have to get to work on time, get the kids to school, and make sure our partner feels loved. Often, this leaves us feeling drained and overwhelmed. By bringing your inner child out to play, you are making space for yourself in the craziness.

That's what it's all about, is it not? Making sure that you have made space for yourself, even the parts that have been closed off for so long. It is easy to forget where we came from; who we used to be. However, these tools are for everyone—wounded or not—who has lost touch with that part of themselves. I hope it has done that for you.

We want to get back to that original part of ourselves, who saw the world through eyes of wonder and never backed down. Reclaiming that piece of ourselves can set us on the path for success. As long as we heal the wounds inflicted upon us and reparent our inner child, we can harness those abilities and move forward into a new day, more confident and full of wonder. After all, the return to childhood is a journey that can give you more benefits than you anticipate.

While the concept of an 'inner child' might have seemed silly at first, I hope that you saw past the buzziness of the phrase and realized it is a helpful and beautiful concept. There are many ways in which this inner child can be of help to you. You will see your self-confidence bloom, and you will see the world through eyes of wonder that you haven't had in quite some time. Despite the purported 'silliness' of the practice, silliness is what it's all about. Being able to throw caution to the wind and take part in some good old-fashioned fun sometimes.

Though, that's not to minimize the wounded inner child that some of you might be suffering from. It is just as important to deal with those early hurts as it is to revel in the fun of childhood. Recognizing trauma and addressing it is not only healthy, it's imperative to living a fully realized life.

The inner child is for everyone to explore— wounded or not. Your childhood is a predecessor of your current state, but it does not have to define you. You are allowed to take the parts that bring you joy and practice them in real time. Go ahead and color. Buy that cute plushie you saw on Etsy. Live a little and let your inner child know that they are seen and heard.

That's really what it is all about—allowing your inner child to feel seen and understood. So many of us are carrying around baggage that we should have put down years ago. There is freedom on the other side when you tap into everything your inner child has in store for you. You just have to take the first step. Then, the next step—and so on. You won't regret the journey and all it will reveal within you.

Though it may seem like it, this need not be a lengthy commitment. Even spending five minutes a day doing things that awaken that child are five minutes well spent. I hope that you utilize the practices in this book that guide you through proper self-care of your inner child.

Self-care is not something to turn up your nose at. It is not self-indulgent; it is necessary to living your best life. It is definitely important to take the time for yourself and make the decision to care for your body and mind. I hope that you continue to practice self-care even after you have finished this book.

We don't need more boring adults that punch the clock and go home to veg out to Netflix. We need adults who have come alive. I believe that finding that inner spark innate in your inner child is right where we should start. Though, you need not always let the inner child take the wheel. It is important to have boundaries, even within oneself. So allow that inner child to come out and play, but make sure that you are acting as parent of those impulses and reining them in when necessary.

You are your own best advocate, so listen to that inner child and show them compassion. You might be surprised at the results. With the tools I have given you, you should be able to reawaken that spark and start living a fuller and more playful life. Go out and use what you have learned. Share with your friends and family. Bring them into the fold and show them how self-compassion can be world changing.

Embrace the journey of others, too, as they learn to acknowledge their inner child. Your relationship will grow in beauty as you both grow together. A relationship built on growth and understanding is a relationship worth sticking out.

More than anything, I hope that you learn how to better connect with the inner child within you and others. This freeing experience can set you on the right path to embracing that which is beautiful within yourself. It can heal old wounds and set your eyes on the horizon with new wonder.

If you appreciated this book and what it has taught you, feel free to leave a review on Amazon. I would greatly appreciate it. I endeavored to make this a book that was worthwhile and informative, so I hope that you enjoyed the journey, and I wish you all the luck. Do not stop here. Continue to pursue this journey. It will be well worth it. Good luck, and have some fun!

REFERENCES

Brown, L. (2020, September 15). *Inner child healing: 7 steps to heal your wounded inner child*. Hack Spirit. https://hackspirit.com/inner-child-healing/

Dean, M. (2022, April 5). *Inner Child: What Is It, What Happened To It, And How Can I Fix It? | Betterhelp*. Www.betterhelp.com. https://www.betterhelp.com/advice/therapy/inner-child-what-is-it-what-happened-to-it-and-how-can-i-fix-it/

Diamond, S. (2008, June 7). *Essential Secrets of Psychotherapy: The Inner Child | Psychology Today*. Www.psychologytoday.com. https://www.psychologytoday.com/us/blog/evil-deeds/200806/essential-secrets-psychotherapy-the-inner-child?amp

Fast, N. (2010, May 13). *How to Stop the Blame Game.* Harvard Business Review. https://hbr.org/2010/05/how-to-stop-the-blame-game

Horton, C. (2018, January 19). *The Pros and Cons of Adulthood.* Charisma's Corner. https://charismas corner.com/the-pros-and-cons-of-adulthood/

Inner child. (2022, April 7). Wikipedia. https://en.m.wikipedia.org/wiki/Inner_child

Jacobsen, S. (2017, March 23). *What is the "Inner Child"?* Harley TherapyTM Blog. https://www.harleytherapy.co.uk/counselling/what-is-the-inner-child.htm

Johnson, E. B. (2020, August 28). *Letting your inner child out to play.* Practical Growth. https://medium.com/practical-growth/letting-your-inner-child-out-d8c48d9fc9f0

Magazine, S. (2021, December 12). *8 Tips for Forgiving Someone Who Hurt You.* Stanfordmag.org. https://stanfordmag.org/contents/8-tips-for-forgiving-someone-who-hurt-you

Mental Health Center. (2019, April 3). *How Childhood Trauma Affects Us As Adults | Mental Health.* Mental Health Center. https://www.mentalhealthcenter.

org/how-childhood-trauma-affects-adult-relationships/

Mintner, K. (2020, May 19). *How to talk to your inner child*. Medium. https://kathrynmintner.medium.com/how-to-talk-to-your-inner-child-de57c8f5f5b0

Paresky, P. (2017, May 5). *Finding Your Inner Adult | Psychology Today*. Www.psychologytoday.com. https://www.psychologytoday.com/us/blog/happiness-and-the-pursuit-leadership/201705/finding-your-inner-adult?amp

Raab, D. (2018, August 6). *Deep Secrets and Inner Child Healing | Psychology Today*. Www.psychologytoday.-com. https://www.psychologytoday.com/us/blog/the-empowerment-diary/201808/deep-secrets-and-inner-child-healing

Smith, M. (2021, October). *Coping with Grief and Loss - HelpGuide.org*. Https://Www.helpguide.org. https://www.helpguide.org/articles/grief/coping-with-grief-and-loss.htm#:~:text=Whatever%20your%20loss%2C%20it

Tams, L. (2013, July 17). *What makes children happy?* MSU Extension. https://www.canr.msu.edu/news/what_makes_children_happy

Trauma and How to Overcome It - The School Of Life. (n.d.). Www.theschooloflife.com. https://www. theschooloflife.com/article/trauma-and-how-to-overcome-it/

Unico, K. (2017, November 6). *Why You Should Love Unapologetically | Her Campus.* Www.hercampus.com. https://www.hercampus.com/school/ucf/why-you-should-love-unapologetically/

Why Healing Your Inner Child is Important. (2021, November 15). G&STC. https://www.gstherapycen ter.com/blog/2019/11/15/why-healing-your-inner-child-is-important#:~:text=Why%20is%20it%20im-portant%20to

Made in the USA
Coppell, TX
08 November 2022

86014099R00104